AF327209

Lake Keitele
A Vision of Finland

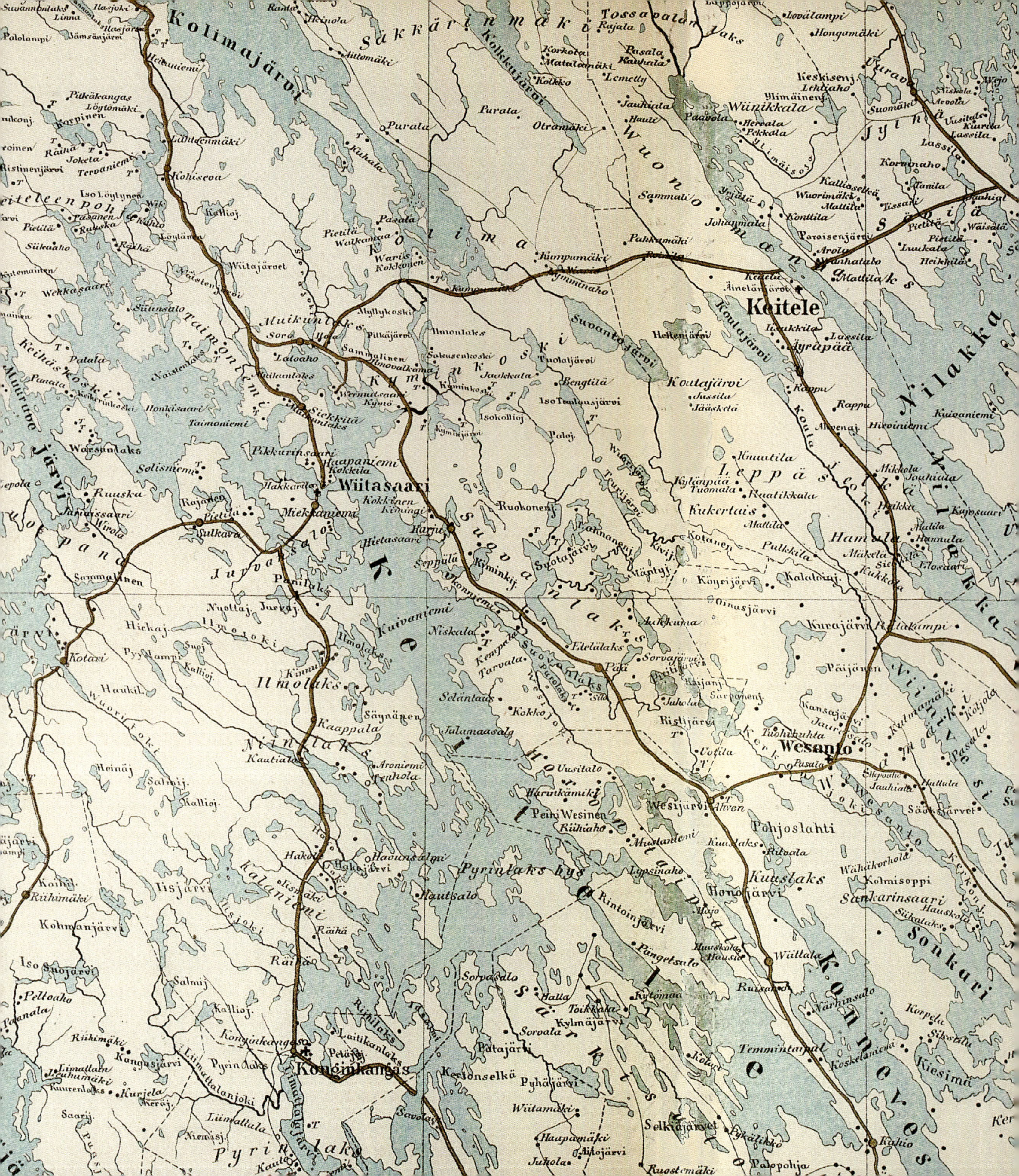

Kolimajärvi
Sakkärinmäki
Tossavaidan laks
Keitele
Wiinikkala
Wuono
Kolima
Nilakka
Jylhä
Wiitasaari
Leppäselkä
Hamula
Kukertais
Konginkangas
Wesanto
Wesijärvi
Kuuslaks
Sonkari
Konnevesi
Pyrinlaks
Juvansalo
Ilmolaks
Niinilaks
Kalaniemi
Ristimäki
Kiesimä

Anne Robbins

Lake Keitele

A Vision of Finland

National Gallery Company, London
Distributed by Yale University Press

Published to accompany the exhibition
Lake Keitele: A Vision of Finland
15 November 2017–4 February 2018

Exhibition generously supported by

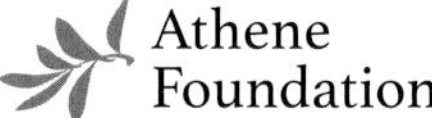 Athene Foundation

With additional support from other donors

This exhibition has been made possible by the provision of insurance through the Government Indemnity Scheme. The National Gallery would like to thank HM Government for providing Government Indemnity and the Department for Culture, Media and Sport and Arts Council England for arranging the indemnity.

First published in Great Britain in 2017 by
National Gallery Company Limited
St Vincent House
30 Orange Street
London WC2H 7HH
www.nationalgallery.co.uk

ISBN: 978 1 85709 624 8
1044763

British Library Cataloguing-in-Publication Data.
A catalogue record is available from the British Library.
Library of Congress Control Number: 2017939577

Publisher: Jan Green
Project Editor: Sophie Kullmann
Publishing Assistant: Elin Sandell
Editor: Linda Schofield
Picture Researcher: Suzanne Bosman
Production: Jane Hyne and Amanda Mackie

Designed by Mark Thomson
Origination by DL Imaging
Printed in Spain by SYL

All measurements give height before width

Front cover: Akseli Gallen-Kallela, *Lake Keitele*, 1905, oil on canvas, 53 × 66 cm, The National Gallery, London (NG6574)

Back cover: Akseli Gallén skiing at the summit of Kirppuvuori in Suolahti, 1906, photograph, Gallen-Kallela Museum, Espoo

Frontispiece: Map of Lake Keitele, plate XVII from *Kartbok Finland* [Atlas of Finland], Tourist Association of Finland, 1897

Contents

Director's Preface   7

Author's Acknowledgements   9

Introduction   11

Catalogue   39

Notes   67
Bibliography   69
List of Lenders   71
Photographic credits   72

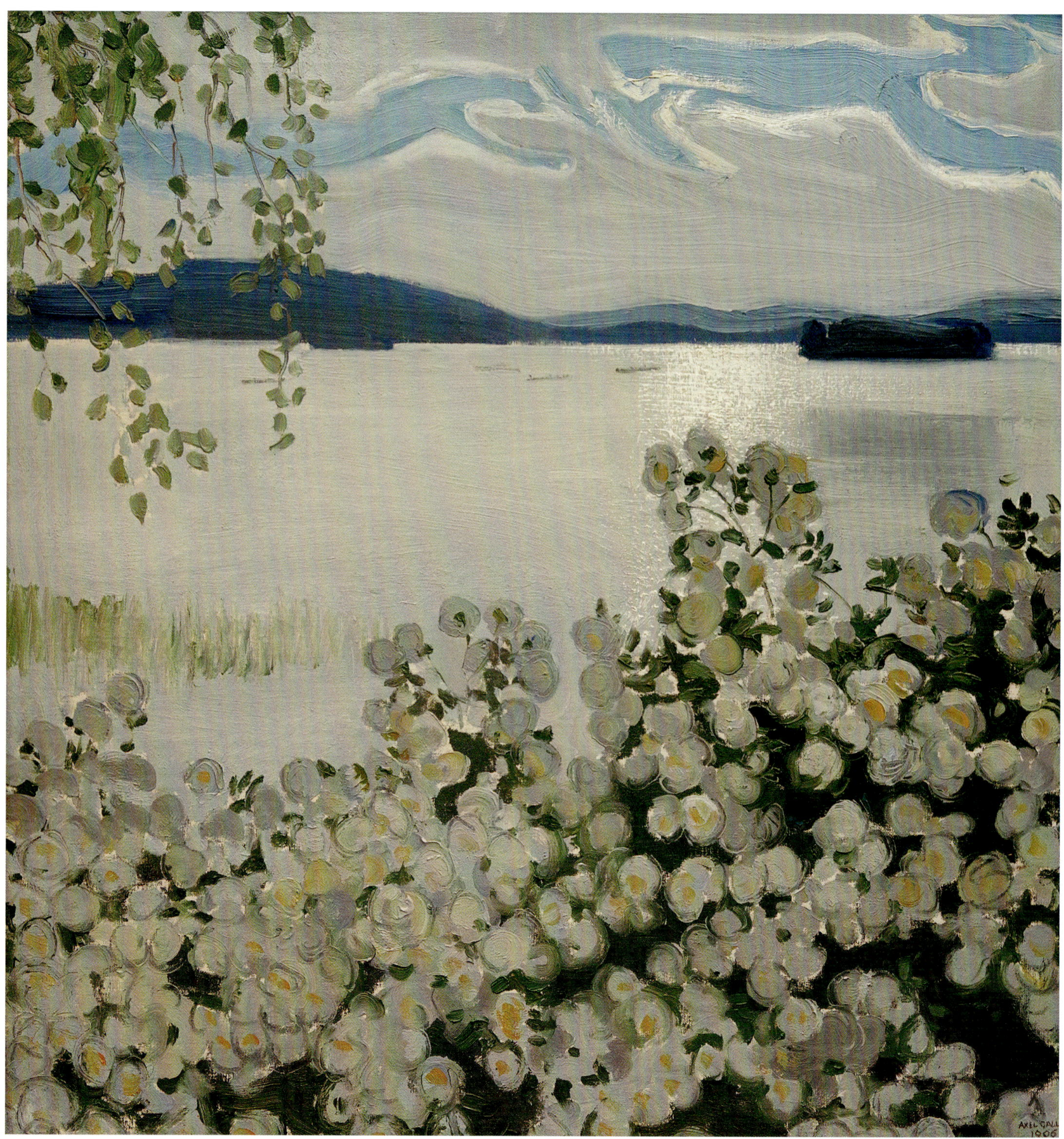

Fig. 1 **Akseli Gallen-Kallela**, *White Roses, Konginkangas*, 1906
Oil on canvas, 62 × 58 cm
Private Collection

Director's Preface

Akseli Gallen-Kallela (1865–1931) is Finland's great national painter. Exactly 100 years ago, in 1917, when he was at the peak of his career and international fame, Finland won its independence from Russia, the culmination of a struggle to which he and his friend and fellow countryman, the composer Jean Sibelius (1865–1957), were deeply committed. Through his paintings of the Finnish landscape and his representations of the *Kalevala* epic, the collection of ancient poems that constitute the foundational myth of Finland, Gallen-Kallela played an important role in defining a visual narrative of nationhood.

Trained in Helsinki and in Paris, very widely travelled in Europe – visiting London in 1895 – and subsequently working as far afield as Nairobi and New Mexico, when he was abroad Gallen-Kallela hankered after the unspoilt beauty and wildness of the Finnish landscape, its dense pine forests on undulating hills and the spectacular cloudscapes shot through with silvery light reflected on the iridescent surface of its numerous lakes. In 1904 Lake Keitele in central Finland cast a quasi-mystical fascination over him as the setting for the imagined passage of the gods and heroes of ancient Finland.

This exhibition, conceived by Anne Robbins, was inspired by the presence in the National Gallery of Gallen-Kallela's painting, *Lake Keitele*, of 1905. Acquired in 1999, it is one of the artist's most eloquent and haunting renditions of the subject and it remains the only painting by him in a public collection in this country. Three other versions of the composition have been brought together to be displayed alongside it, as well as a carefully selected group of other lake subjects, including *Väinämöinen with Maidens*, which shows the heroic bard of the *Kalevala* departing for his final adventures.

We are grateful to all the lenders, both private and institutional, who have readily and generously made their works available to us. We are grateful to the Finnish Embassy in London and Suomi 100 for assistance and encouragement. It is a pleasure to thank the Athene Foundation and the other supporters who have made this exhibition possible.

Gabriele Finaldi

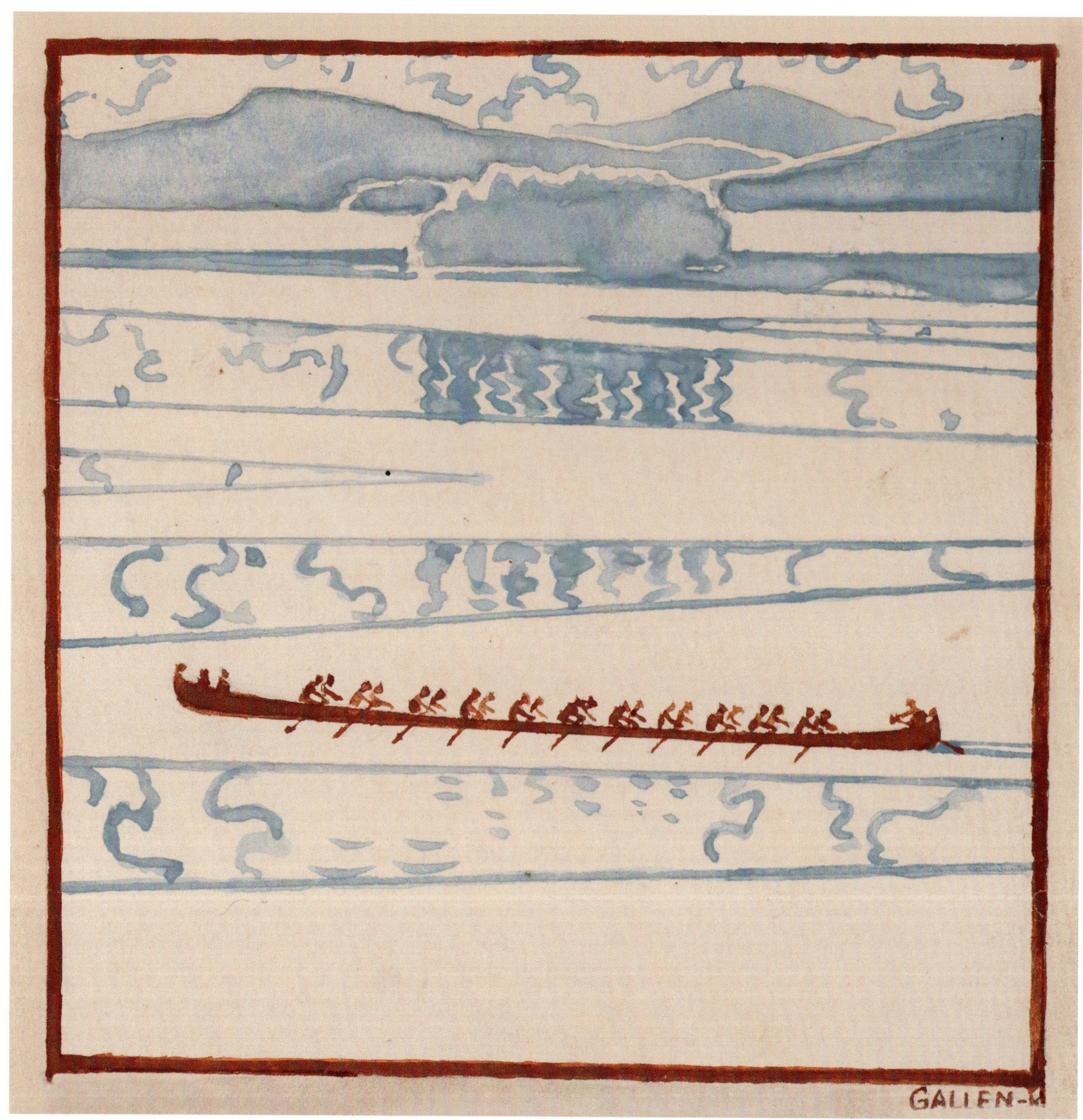

Fig. 2 **Akseli Gallen-Kallela**, *Lake Sketch for the Great Kalevala*, 1920
Watercolour on paper, 12.5 × 12.5 cm
Gallen-Kallela Museum, Espoo

Author's Acknowledgements

This exhibition and catalogue would not have been possible without the support of Gabriele Finaldi, Director of the National Gallery, to whom I am profoundly grateful. For their trust and constant encouragement I would like to thank Jane Knowles and Caroline Campbell; the preparation of this catalogue has benefited from the latter's insightful comments. This study is crucially beholden to Christopher Riopelle, who almost two decades ago was instrumental in the acquisition of Gallen-Kallela's *Lake Keitele* for the National Gallery: a brilliant, pioneering addition to the collection and the starting point for this exhibition. He supported the genesis and development of this project from the beginning and provided vital assistance. This publication has benefited from the expertise and attentive care of Jan Green, Jane Hyne, Suzanne Bosman and Elin Sandell, and Sophie Kullmann, whom I thank for her unflinching enthusiasm. Mark Thomson designed this stunning book; I thank him warmly. My deepest thanks also go to Sunnifa Hope, for her invaluable help.

This exhibition is indebted to Suzanne Pagé's remarkable shows on Nordic art; it was inspired by her groundbreaking reunion of the four versions of Gallen-Kallela's *Lake Keitele* at the Fondation Louis Vuitton, Paris, in 2015. I am also grateful to Adrian Biddell for his constant support and helpful suggestions.

For their ever-friendly, energetic assistance, I would especially like to thank Minna Turtiainen and Tuija Wahlroos at the Gallen-Kallela Museum, who provided inestimable help, generously sharing their knowledge and expertise. The exhibition and this book owe a great deal to their unrivalled scholarship. I also owe a debt to Janne Gallen-Kallela-Sirén, who early on gave advice and insight.

My gratitude goes to the institutions that have generously lent to this exhibition and to the directors and curators of those collections who facilitated my visits to study their works of art: at the Finnish National Gallery, Susanna Pettersson, Anna-Maria von Bonsdorff, Teijamari Jyrkkiö; at the Didrichsen Museum, Peter Didrichsen, Maria Didrichsen, Otto Selén; at the Lahti Art Museum, Timo Simanainen, Maija-Ritta Kallio; and Mikael Schnitt at Hagelstam & Co. I also thank the collectors who wish to remain anonymous, as well as the following individuals, who assisted me in various ways: Giovanna Bertazzoni, Rickie Burman, Marie-Monique Couvegnes, Gill Hart, Pekka Huhtaniemi, Leah Kharibian, Thomas Knöll, Carlo Knöll, Patrick O'Sullivan, Pirjo Pellinen, Jussi Pylkkänen and Stuart Wrede. I thank Luc, Edgar and Gabriel for their patience.

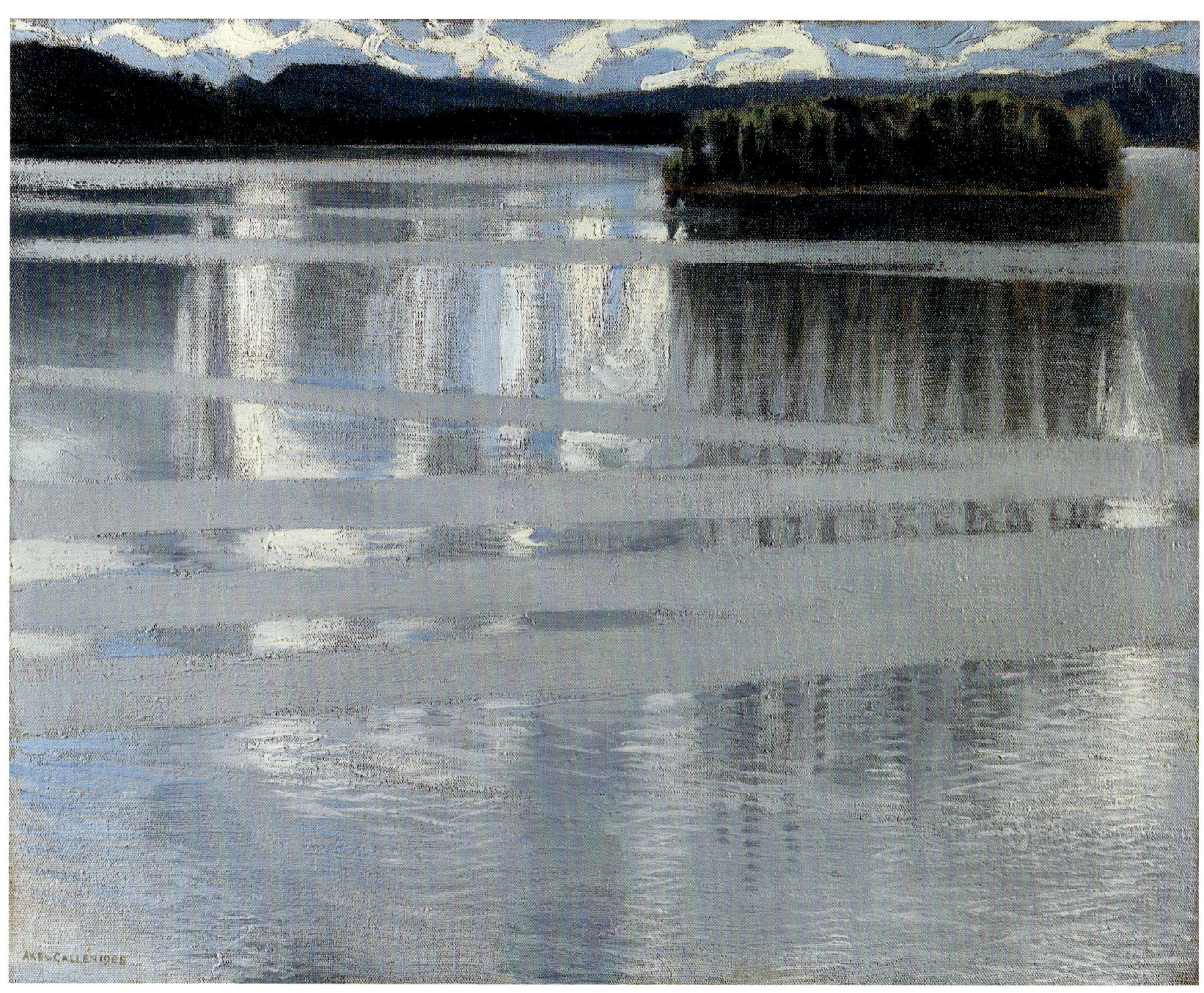

Cat. 7   **Akseli Gallen-Kallela**, *Lake Keitele*, 1905
Oil on canvas, 53 × 66 cm
The National Gallery, London

Introduction

Since its acquisition in 1999, *Lake Keitele* (cat. 7) has become one of the best-loved and most familiar paintings in the National Gallery. Painted by the Finnish artist Akseli Gallen-Kallela (1865–1931) in 1905, depicting the eponymous lake in central Finland, it is not an obvious popular favourite; this is the only Finnish work of art in the collection and the artist is not familiar to the British public. Part of the painting's appeal lies in its apparent simplicity and serenity as a landscape. Yet properly understood in its historic context, Gallen-Kallela's creation stands at the crossroads of several genres and categories: landscape and mythology; political statement and inner, psychologically charged vision; primitivism and near-abstraction. It has been called one of the most emblematic Nordic landscapes of its time.[1]

The *Lake Keitele* now in the National Gallery Collection is actually one of four pictures of this subject by Gallen-Kallela, painted between 1904 and 1906, just over a decade before Finland became a fully independent state, in the wake of the Russian Revolutions of 1917. Part of the Kingdom of Sweden for almost seven centuries, and from 1809 an autonomous Grand Duchy of the Russian Empire, in the years around 1900 Finland sought to assert an independent cultural identity. Gallen-Kallela played a key role in defining the visual culture of the evolving nation. Many of his works reflect the newly rediscovered legends of ancient Finland, particularly the great epic poem, the *Kalevala*, compiled by Elias Lönnrot, and first published in 1835. For this reason, and despite their modest scale, some modern critics have claimed the Lake Keitele landscapes as Gallen-Kallela's contribution to the 'constructed image of an unborn nation'.[2]

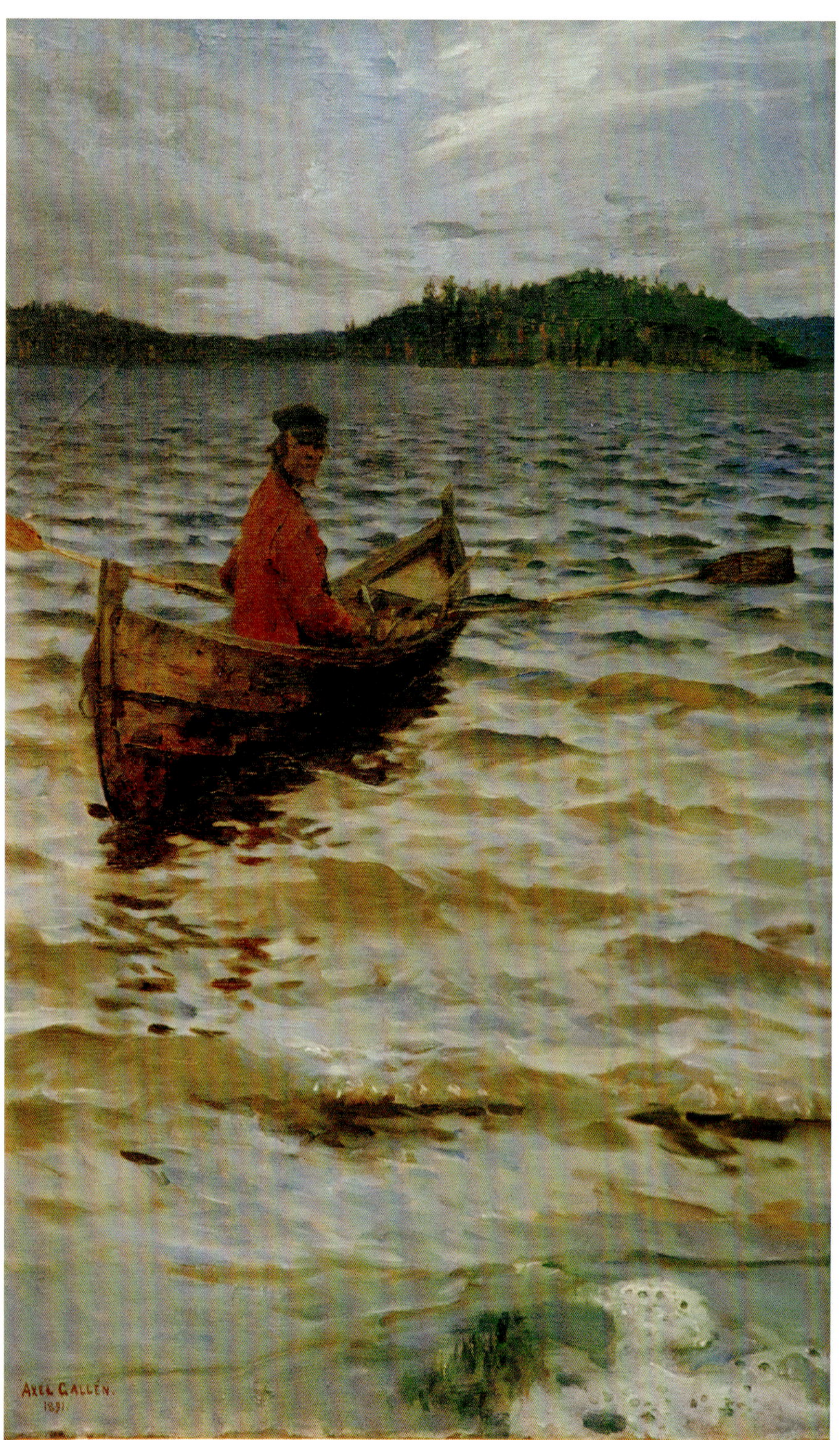

Fig. 3 **Akseli Gallen-Kallela**, *Rowing to the Shore*
(Soutaja), 1891
Oil on canvas, 64 × 40 cm
Serlachius Fine Arts Foundation, Mänttäa

More recently, Gallen-Kallela's views have also been claimed as embodiments of 'modern' art with a particularly Nordic twist. In 2015, the National Gallery's *Lake Keitele* featured in the inaugural exhibition of the Fondation Louis Vuitton in Paris, as a painting which – together with key works by Pablo Picasso, Henri Matisse, Claude Monet, Kazimir Malevich, Alberto Giacometti and Francis Bacon (the acknowledged artistic giants of the first half of the twentieth century) – laid the foundations of modern art, consciously rejecting the academic art traditions of the past. This introduction examines the many different ways in which this painting can be understood and contextualised.

Akseli Gallen-Kallela: origins and influences

Born in Pori, a small port on the Gulf of Bothnia, western Finland, in 1865, Akseli Gallen-Kallela was the son of a local chief of police and cashier at the Bank of Finland, and his childhood was spent in the nearby Tyrvää region. There he enjoyed a simple, rural way of life, amid a preserved, uncorrupted nature. His schooling took him to the Finnish capital Helsinki, first to the Swedish Grammar School, where he also attended evening arts and crafts classes, and then, from 1881, to the city's private and public art academies. Albert Edelfelt (1854–1905), one of the most influential exponents of Realism and plein-air painting (painting outdoors) in Finland, tutored him in 1883–4. Edelfelt had encountered success at the Paris Salon with ambitious history, genre and landscape paintings, and it was to Paris that Gallen-Kallela also travelled to continue his artistic education, the fortunate recipient of a series of scholarships from the Finnish Senate; the young country boy was already showing much promise.

Gallen-Kallela spent five years in the French capital, living there intermittently, studying first at the Académie Julian and later at the Atelier Cormon.[3] He joined a lively community of fellow Finns, Danes, Norwegians and Swedes eager to pursue their art or perfect their technique in the French capital, such as his friends Carl Dørnberger, Erik Järnefelt and August Strindberg. Paris was considered an important platform not just for artistic training, but also for showing one's work, an essential first step for any artist determined to make their name.

At the Paris Salon, where Gallen-Kallela became a regular exhibitor from as early as 1886, Finnish art was fashionable, praised for its ingenuity and freshness. The artist encountered success, advancing his reputation both in France and in his native Finland, winning numerous awards and medals, and later the commission for murals and interiors for the Finnish Pavilion at the Paris World Fair (Exposition Universelle) of 1900. These fertile years in Paris immersed Gallen-Kallela in the international art world and were crucial for shaping his career. In the following decade he increasingly sent works to a number of exhibitions outside of Finland, notably a show in Berlin in 1895 arranged jointly with the Norwegian painter Edvard Munch, and the *Mir Iskusstva* (World of Art) exhibition organised by Sergei Diaghilev in St Petersburg in 1899 (in which Finnish artists had been encouraged to participate by Edelfelt, for diplomatic reasons). These shows raised Gallen-Kallela's profile, triggering more invitations and commissions from public institutions and private collectors.

Gallen-Kallela's style evolved, stimulated by this range of Finnish and foreign influences. His early paintings show the impact of Edelfelt's works, although they are not as anecdotal and contain less obvious narrative content. During his Paris years, paintings by the French Realist Jules Bastien-Lepage (1848–1884), which he saw at the posthumous exhibition of the artist's work in 1885, made a strong impact on Gallen-Kallela, with their high horizon lines and dry, controlled brushwork. In addition, he learnt the art of rigorous composition in the studio of his one-time master, William Bouguereau (1825–1905). Both these characteristics are evident in the Lake Keitele landscapes. Embedded in the natural environment, with a quintessentially Finnish subject matter, they are also indebted to the latest developments in French painting. With its simplified forms and absence of shadows, *Lake Keitele* is not without affinity with the aesthetic of the School of Pont-Aven, many of whose artists were inspired by the works of Paul Gauguin. Gallen-Kallela's Finnish friends Pekka Halonen and Väinö Blomsted had both studied painting under Gauguin for a short time in Paris. Blomsted's *Sunset* (1898), with its daring composition and its flat, harshly contrasted areas of colour, has a synthetic, unrealistic appearance that harks back to Gauguin.

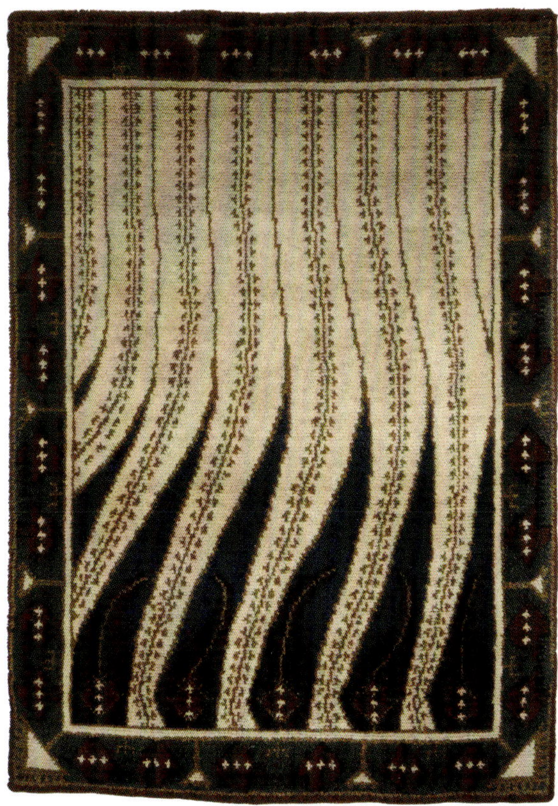

Fig. 4 **Akseli Gallen-Kallela**, *Liekkiryijy* ('Flame' rug), 1965
Replica of 1900 original
Textile (wool)
Gallen-Kallela Museum, Espoo

Gallen-Kallela and the applied arts

Lake Keitele also brings to mind the art of stained glass, eschewing modelling and borrowing from this type of artwork its severe, firm-lined, 'cloisonné' motif. Gallen-Kallela's interest in stained glass had developed during a visit to London in 1895. At the British Museum he admired Celtic manuscripts, but the medieval stained glass he saw at the South Kensington Museum (now the Victoria and Albert Museum) made an especially strong impression. This prompted him to buy his own glass furnace, which he had delivered (together with a printing press) to his wilderness studio at Kalela, where he soon tried his hand at these techniques (see cat. 2). *Lake Keitele*, with its flattened space and unmodulated areas of colour, bears testimony to Gallen-Kallela's knowledge and practice of the art of stained glass, while also evoking the artist's textile creations. The most celebrated of these is his 'Flame' rug: a *ryjiy* or woven rug designed by Gallen-Kallela for the Finnish pavilion of the Paris World Fair of 1900. The rug was decorated with a naturalistic motif of ferns, read upside down as flames (fig. 4). This finds an echo in the graphic, decorative lines and asymmetric dynamism of the Lake Keitele landscapes.[4]

Gallen-Kallela excelled in the applied arts and traditional crafts, to which he had been introduced when he was growing up in Finland. He claimed he would never take on a pupil or apprentice who could not carve a decent axe handle.[5] He was a talented carpenter, and also accomplished in metalwork and furniture-making, as well as with stained glass and textiles; his skills were further honed during the construction of his studio house, built to his design in a magnificent setting in Ruovesi, central Finland, started in 1894. This house, called Kalela, was a *Gesamtkunstwerk* (a complete work of art) of his own creation, for which Gallen-Kallela designed and carved details ranging from door handles to clothes pegs. He even sculpted his own skis, for 'powder snow', in what he described as 'Kallela style'[6]: a variation on the Finnish folk motifs he had collected in Karelia during his honeymoon, and also influenced by the international Arts and Crafts movement of which this well-travelled artist was very much aware.

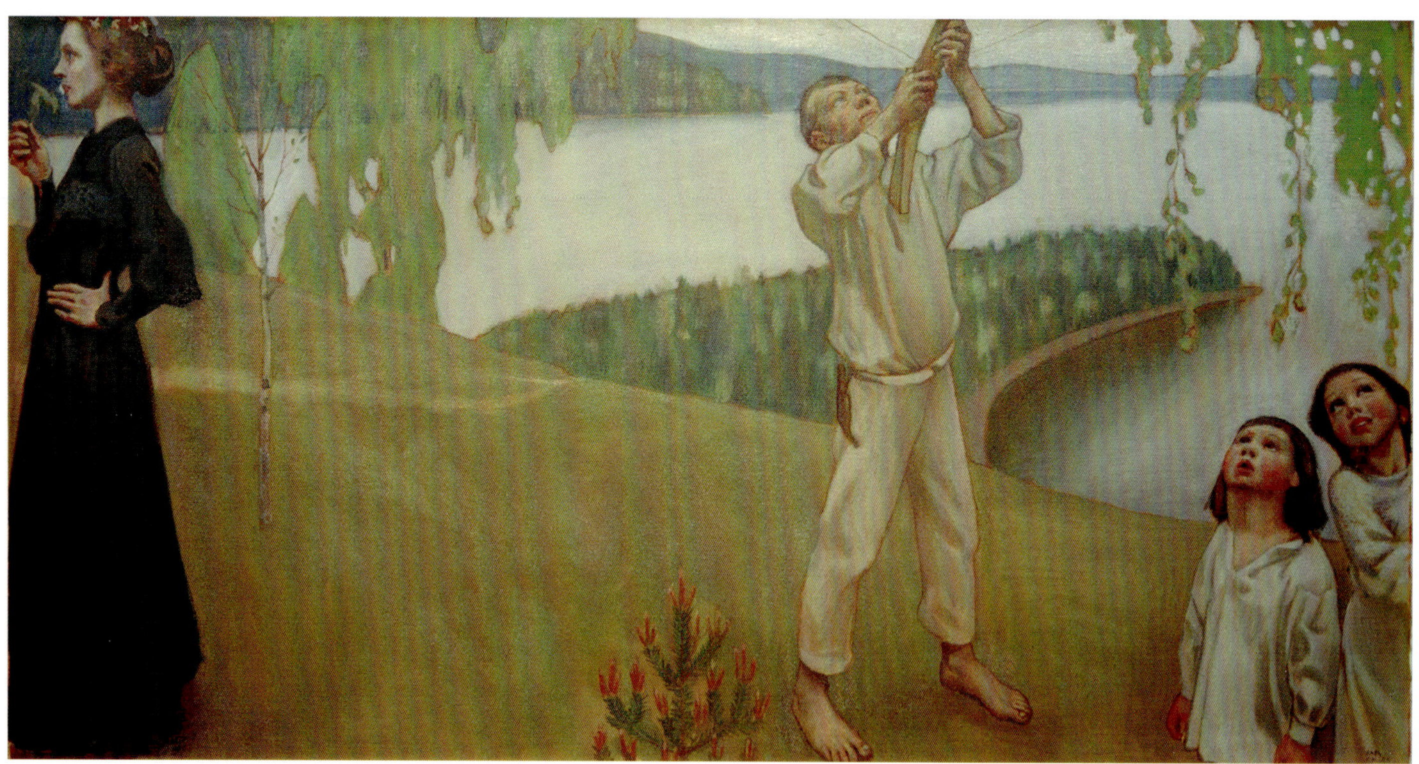

Fig. 5 **Akseli Gallen-Kallela**, *Spring*,
Study for the Jusélius Mausoleum frescoes, 1903
Oil on canvas, 77 × 145 cm
Finnish National Gallery, Ateneum Art Museum, Helsinki

A creative crisis

The simplification of Gallen-Kallela's visual language, evident in *Lake Keitele*, was brought about by his assimilation of international trends, his knowledge of local Finnish crafts and his experimentation in the applied arts. It culminated in the first years of the twentieth century with a series of frescoes commissioned by a Finnish industrialist, Fritz Arthur Jusélius. These were to decorate the walls of a mausoleum in the city of Pori for Jusélius's daughter, Sigrid, who had died at the age of 11 (Gallen-Kallela had also suffered the tragic loss of a child; in 1895 his first daughter, Impi Marjatta, died from diphtheria). The project proved time- and energy-consuming, as well as challenging, even though Gallen-Kallela had studied early Renaissance and ancient Roman frescoes on a trip to Italy in 1898, and had mastered that particular technique. It also brought much frustration: fresco is best suited to wall decoration in a warm Mediterranean climate, but because of the poor environmental conditions in the mausoleum, the paintings started to deteriorate only months after the completion of the whole cycle in 1903; in 1931, the frescoes were destroyed by fire (fig. 5). Their theme, a meditation on life and death, prompted Gallen-Kallela to question the enduring nature of all art, including his own. At that point, in his late 30s and at the height of his career, Gallen-Kallela fell prey to discouragement. Amid this creative crisis he contemplated returning to Paris to draw life models, and fantasised about 'start[ing] over, like a school boy'.[7]

Lake Keitele: a psychological landscape?

The early months of 1904 were a restless, unsettled period for Gallen-Kallela, following the completion of the ill-fated Jusélius frescoes. He spent the first part of that year away from Finland, firstly in Vienna, then travelling with his wife to Milan, Monte-Carlo and finally to Granada in the south of Spain. There the exhausted artist contracted malaria; back in Finland he recuperated. Gallen-Kallela and his family rented a summer lodge in Konginkangas, on the shores of Lake Keitele, which was more practical for the convalescing artist than his remote studio house in Ruovesi.

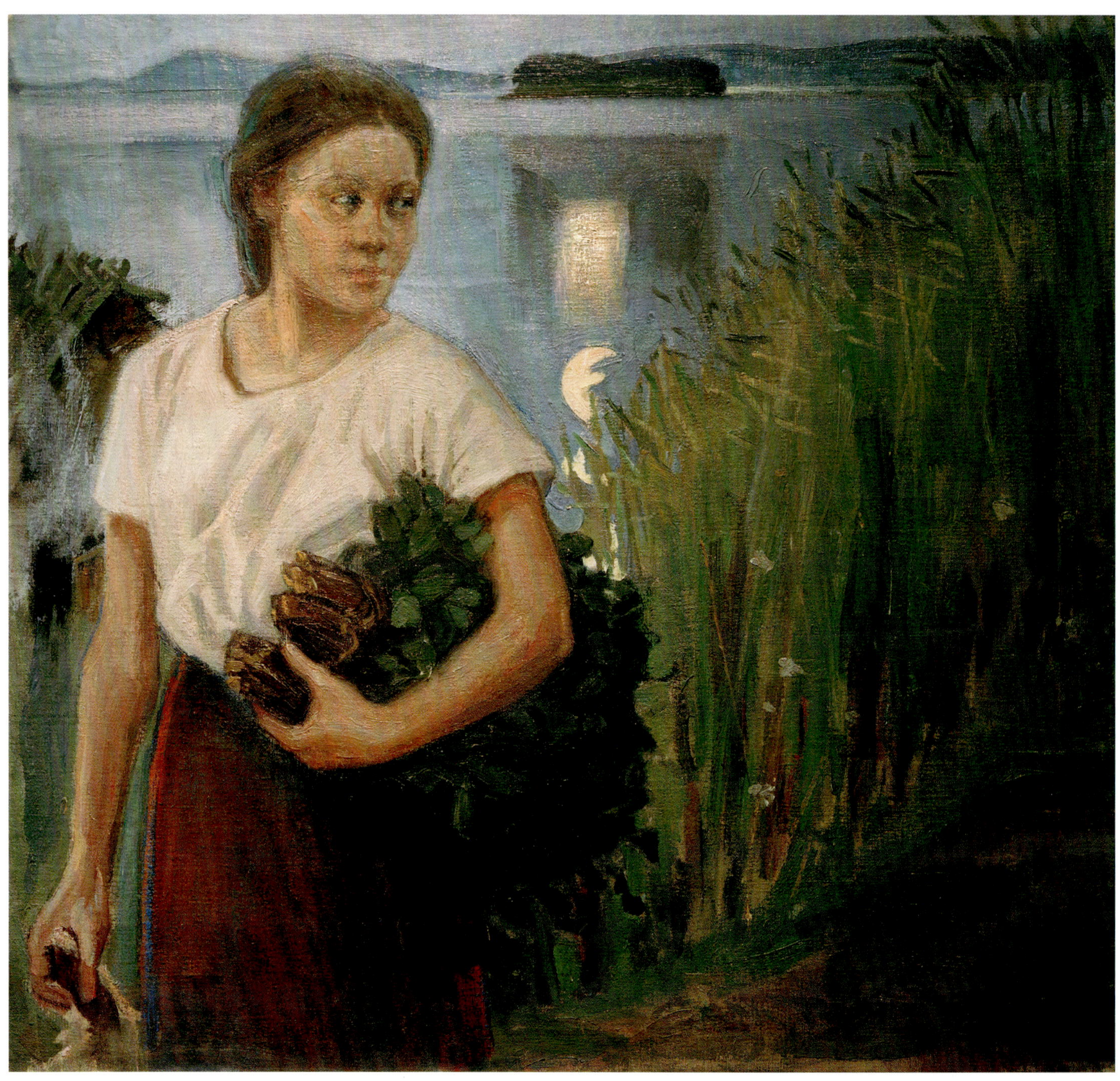

Fig. 6 **Akseli Gallen-Kallela**, *The Sauna Girl*, 1904
Oil on canvas, 98 × 67 cm
Private collection

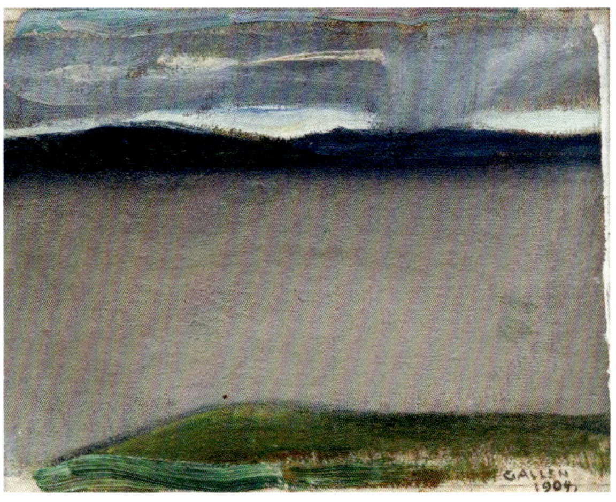

Fig. 7 **Akseli Gallen-Kallela**, *Landscape*, 1904
Oil on canvas on board, 21 × 27 cm
Private collection

The Finnish countryside – its forests, lakes and islands – had always stimulated Gallen-Kallela, and throughout his career it served to revive his creative energies. 'I am terribly lonely in "gay" Paris', he wrote in 1888 from the French capital to a friend in Finland, 'I think of you with envy as you fill your lungs with the fresh country air'.[8] In general, he would alternate between stays in Paris and long periods in his native country, each time retreating to the Finnish countryside with the same sense of wonder: 'Is it the silence of the wilderness that so enchants me?' he pondered in a letter to Mary Slöör, his future wife, in 1888.[9] Country folk and the rugged, barren Finnish landscapes (often dominated by lakes, fig. 3), like those he encountered in 1890 during his honeymoon trip to Karelia, in eastern Finland, provided him with a myriad of subjects to paint: 'It is wild and very beautiful here, a vast wilderness untouched by human hands. There are no farms in these parts, only […] tall mighty pines. The pinewoods unfold as far as the eye can see, across a landscape of hills, swamps and lakes'.[10]

Lintula Villa, the site of Gallen-Kallela's convalescence in 1904, sat on the edge of Lake Keitele at Lintulahti bay, part of the Lake Päijänne waterway, and offered glorious views stretching out to the horizon. In a series of freely executed and informal pictures, he painted his wife, Mary, against the Lake Keitele backdrop (cat. 4) and also posed a local girl carrying branches to a sauna (fig. 6); believed to be 17-year-old Roosa Honkonen, daughter of the tenant farmer of Lintula Villa. The Lake Keitele landscapes must have been started during this same period. A surviving small, wonderfully spontaneous study (fig. 7) testifies to Gallen-Kallela's direct observation of the motif, which he was then to develop in his studio.

The artist had adopted the practice of sketching outside when a student of Albert Edelfelt 20 years earlier, and did so regardless of the sometimes challenging weather conditions to be found in the Finnish countryside. 'I have been working outdoors, painting a dazzling snowscape, but the weather is so bitterly cold that I am forced to keep dashing indoors to thaw out my palette', he noted in February 1887.[11] His years in Paris no doubt systematised this approach: he would have become fully acquainted with the Realist trends dominant in the painting studios where he studied, which encouraged artists to base their representations of the natural world on studies made out of doors, *en plein air*.

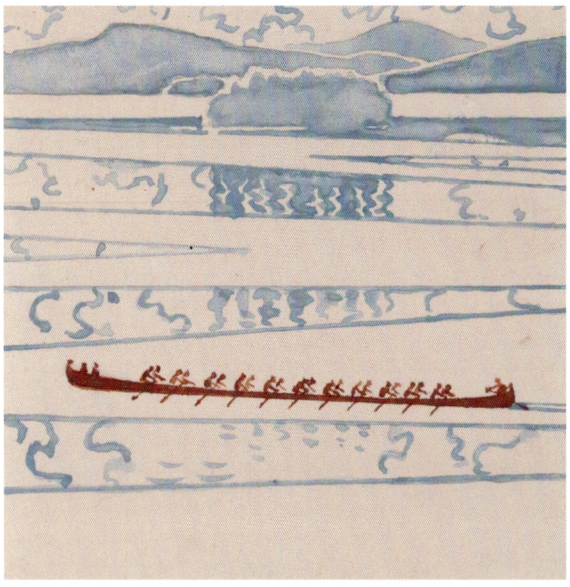

Fig. 8 **Akseli Gallen-Kallela**, *Lake Sketch for the Great Kalevala*, 1920
Watercolour on paper, 12.5 × 12.5 cm
Gallen-Kallela Museum, Espoo

The Lake Keitele pictures bear the weight of creative doubts and carry a psychological dimension. In Gallen-Kallela's landscapes, elements of nature possess their own character, each of them reflecting human feelings and man's inner world: the infinitely varied states of the mind are mirrored in the natural environment. Although a celebration of the beauty of nature, the Lake Keitele landscapes exude a sense of silence and isolation. The vast expanse of water, a characteristic Symbolist subject, projects ethereal reflections; a distant, mysterious island casts a sombre shadow on the glittering surface of the lake, imbuing the composition with a meditative quality.

The powerful visual impact of *Lake Keitele* may stem from its balance between stillness and motion: the immensity and immobility of a landscape bathed in an idealistic, frozen radiance that even a boat crossing the lake, as added by the artist in his later reiterations of the motif, fails to disturb (figs 8 and 9). Yet the pictures are given dynamism by the prominent, almost abstract zigzag that invites the eye to dive into the image and climb up its ladder of diagonal lines to reach the horizon. This geometric form is made of clear fields of paint, applied with a broad brush dragged from one side of the canvas to the other, drawing attention to the artistic process itself rather than the subject of the work. These lines create an illusion of depth, and they endow the painting with a rich narrative content that turns the prosaic landscape into a legendary setting. Gallen-Kallela had previously used this strategy in one of his most important and complex works, *Waterfall at Mäntykoski* (1893), the largest single canvas he ever painted, and one of his Symbolist masterpieces (fig. 10). In this composition, an enormous, realistic landscape is bisected by five straight vertical lines, like the taut strings of an instrument, suggesting a musical echo to the waterfall, its melody pervading the landscape. In *Lake Keitele*, likewise, Gallen-Kallela employs the abstract lines and heavy masses of the grey streaks on the water to convey his own feeling for nature, and his questioning about its artistic representation.

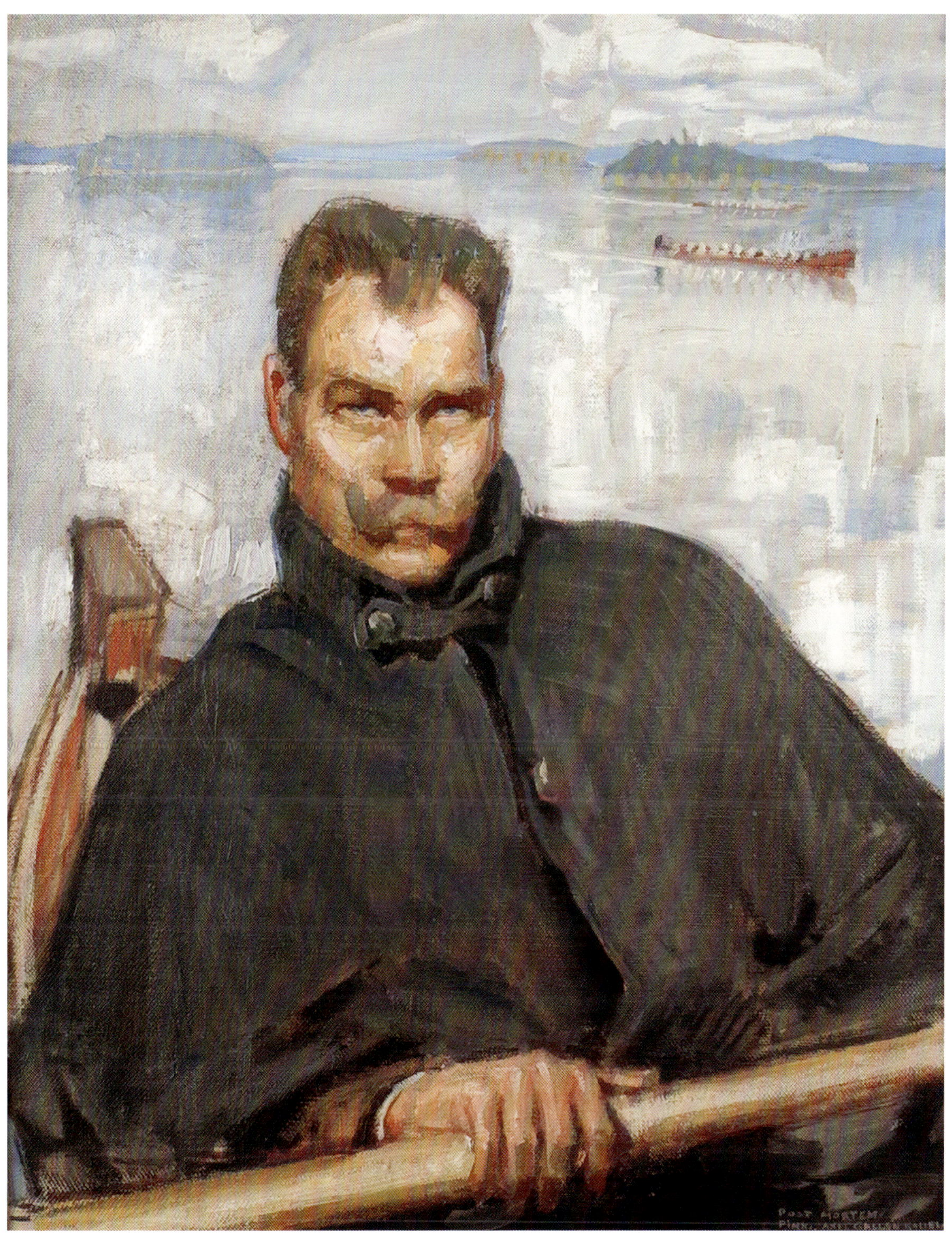

Fig. 9   **Akseli Gallen-Kallela**, *Portrait of the author Johannes Linnankoski*, 1923
Oil on canvas, 85 × 65 cm
Werner Söderström Literary Foundation, Helsinki

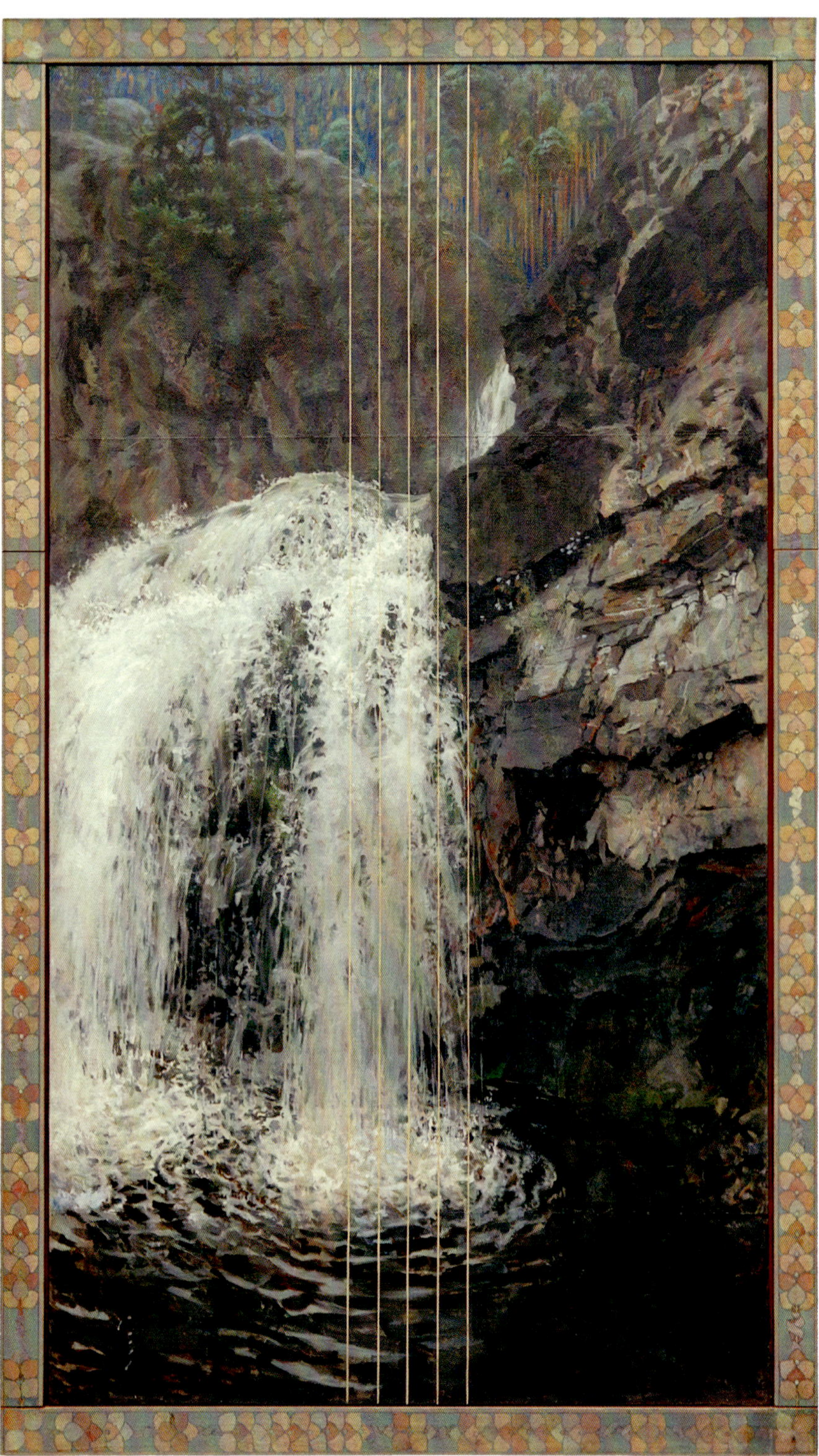

Fig. 10 **Akseli Gallen-Kallela**, *Waterfall at Mäntykoski*, 1892–94
Oil on canvas, 270 × 156 cm
Private collection

Lake Keitele: artistic precedents

Lake Keitele also harks back to other images of departures to faraway shores, such as the *Pilgrimage to Cythera* (1717) by Antoine Watteau, an allegorical voyage to or from an island of love where the light, dreamy mood is tinged with melancholy. Gallen-Kallela may have seen this painting at the Musée du Louvre during one of his many visits to Paris. Another precedent is Arnold Böcklin's *The Island of the Dead*, in which a boat glides towards a tall enigmatic island, carrying a figure reminiscent of Charon ferrying the souls of the dead to Hades (fig. 11). Böcklin was revered by many avant-garde painters, and this image was circulated widely. Gallen-Kallela paraphrased Böcklin's picture in his own *The Island of Dreams*, the two versions of which show a dark, threatening mass of land emerging from the sea in the twilight (fig. 12). Another work with extraordinary resonance in avant-garde circles at the turn of the century, and a key image of international Symbolism, was Puvis de Chavannes's *The Poor Fisherman* (fig. 13). With its muted tones and eerie, bleak atmosphere, the painting had sparked controversy at the Paris Salon in 1881, and again in 1887, when Gallen-Kallela may have seen it.[12] He would have been impressed by its formal qualities: the flat, solid surface of the water establishes a distance from reality and likens it to a mirage.

Fig. 11   **Arnold Böcklin**, *The Island of the Dead*, 1880
Oil on canvas, 111 × 155 cm
Kunstmuseum Basel

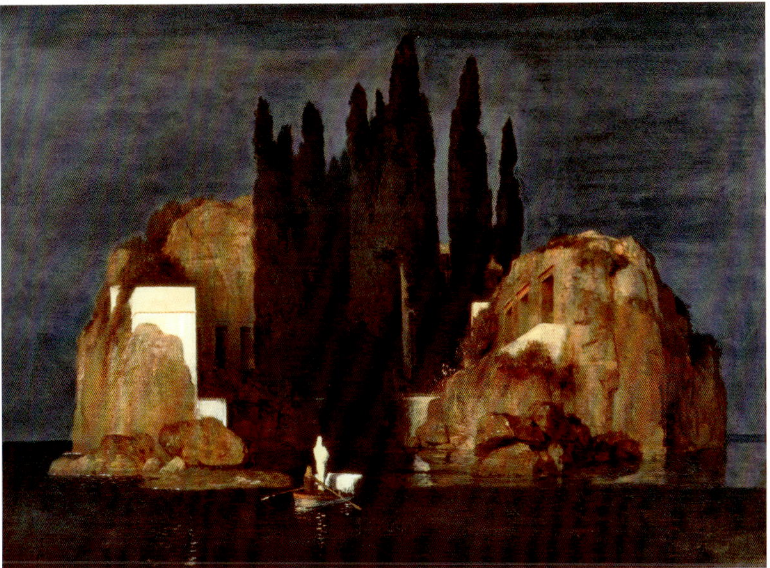

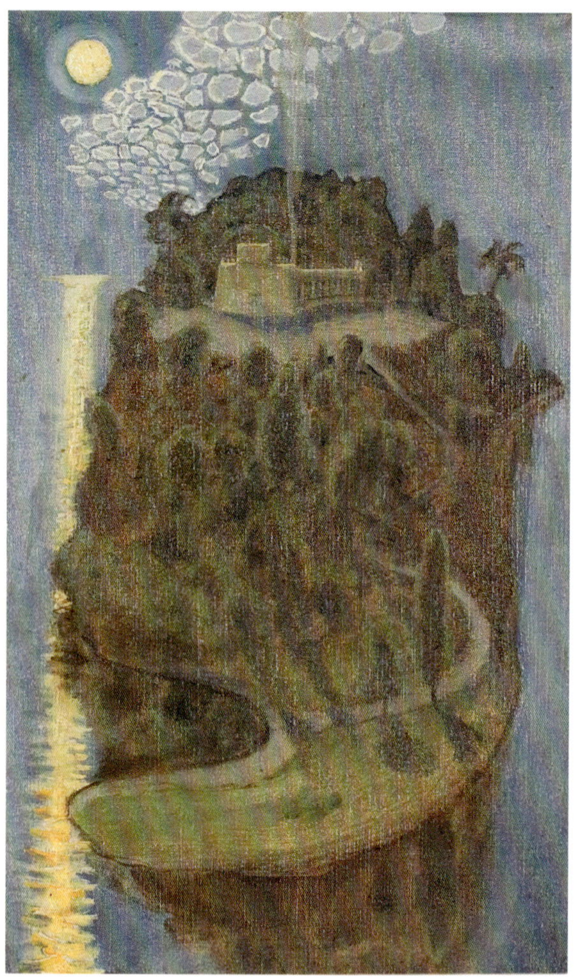

Fig. 12 **Akseli Gallen-Kallela**, *The Island of Dreams*, 1897
Tempera on canvas, 25 × 16 cm
Private collection; on deposit in the Gallen-Kallela Museum,
Espoo

Lake Keitele: pure landscape

In contrast, however, to these works by Watteau, Böcklin and Puvis, the reflective, meditative mood of the Lake Keitele pictures is in each case conveyed by the strength of the landscape alone, without the support of figures to build a narrative. The singular grey bands that play across the surface of the water result from a climatic phenomenon caused by the wind, which delineates an astonishing zigzag interrupting the silvery reflections. The pictorial potential of this natural occurrence had been noted by landscape painters before Gallen-Kallela. John Brett, an English painter associated with the Pre-Raphaelites who was fascinated by weather effects and meteorological variations, made it the focus of an ambitious, large-scale seascape of 1871 (fig. 14). This effect was often observed on Finnish lakes. For Gallen-Kallela these luminous streaks became 'Väinämöinen's wake', thus comparing them with the shimmering trace left by Väinämöinen, one of the main characters in the Finnish epic *Kalevala*, who we are meant to imagine has just rowed past. By inviting this particular interpretation of the painting, the artist conferred an additional mythical layer to a picture seemingly embedded in reality, endowing it with further depth and meaning.

Lake Keitele and the *Kalevala*

The *Kalevala* is a collection of Finnish and Karelian folk poems, or runes, some of them millennia-old. They were passed down the generations as songs, and were compiled by Elias Lönnrot and published in Finland in 1835 for the first time; an extended version followed in 1849. To this day, the *Kalevala* remains a defining element of Finland's cultural identity, extolling the mythical origins of the land. From the mid-nineteenth century artists increasingly found inspiration in the stories of the *Kalevala* and the deeds of its heroes, characterised by their human weakness and divine wisdom: its legends embody universal feelings of hatred and love, remorse or revenge. Gallen-Kallela felt a deep affinity for the main figures of these mythological and heroic tales, which start with an account of the creation. The world of the *Kalevala* is populated by wizards, bards and magi, including Ilmarinen, the smith and forger of the Sampo, a magical tool capable of grinding wheat, making coins and

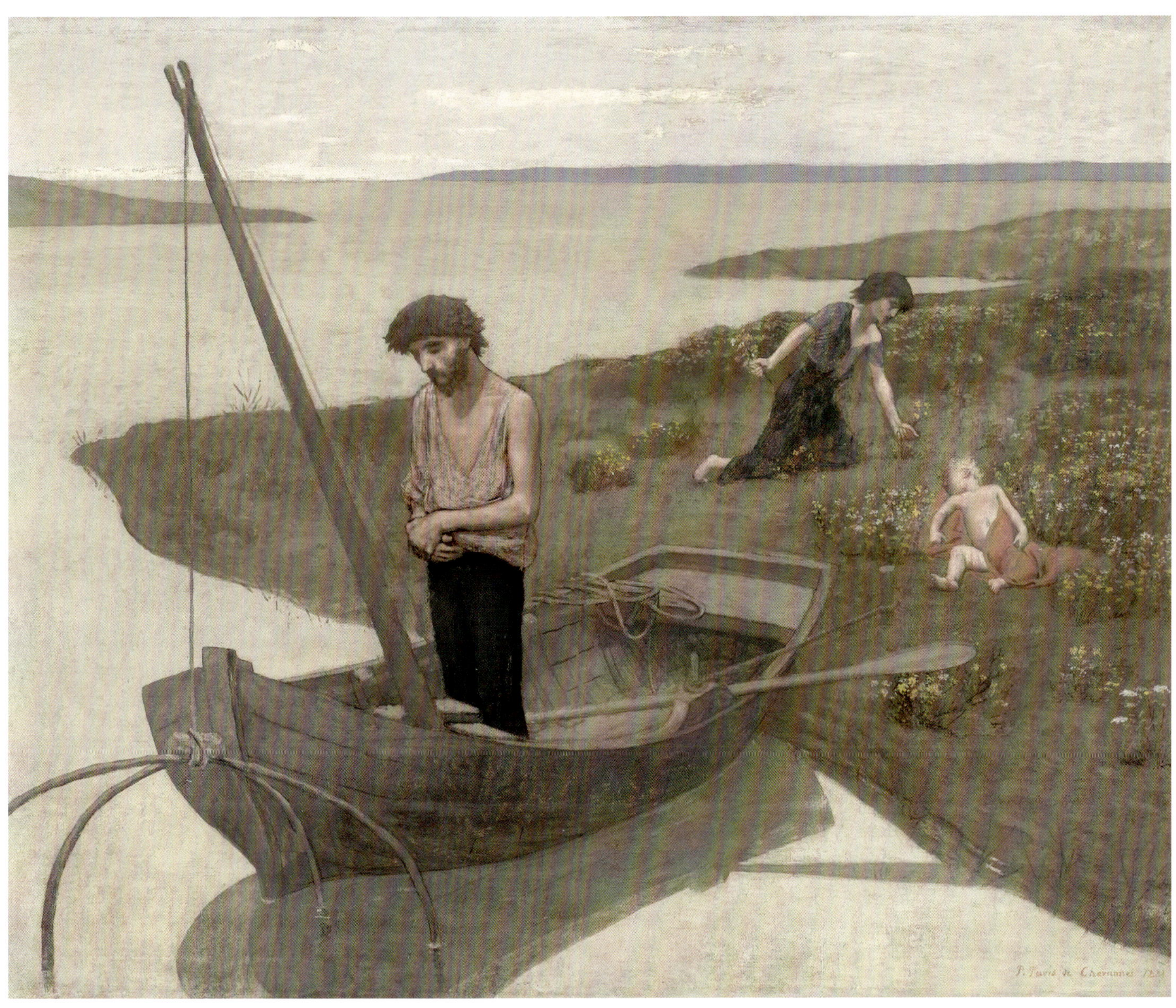

Fig. 13   **Puvis de Chavannes**, *The Poor Fisherman*, 1881
Oil on canvas, 155.5 × 192.5 cm
Musée d'Orsay, Paris

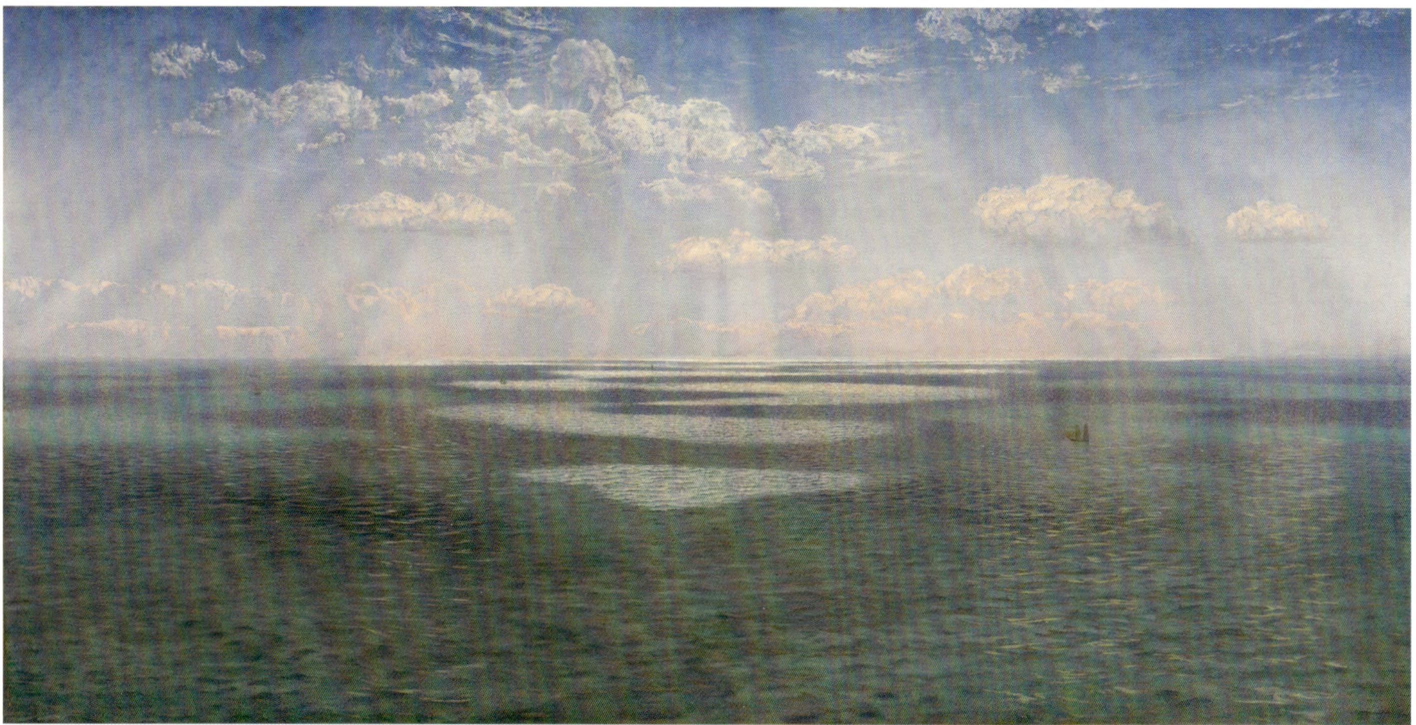

Fig. 14   **John Brett**, *The British Channel Seen from the Dorsetshire Cliffs*, 1871
Oil on canvas, 106 × 212.7 cm
Tate, London

bringing luck; Lemminkäinen, the wild adventurer; Kullervo, the bold, unlucky warrior; Joukahainen, the singer; and Väinämöinen, the wise old man, fisherman, builder of boats, singer and enchanter. The latter is a once-and-future presence in the Lake Keitele landscapes: out of sight, he has just departed, but the silvery wake of his boat bears the promise of his return. The paintings thus allude to Rune 50 of the *Kalevala*, which tells of Väinämöinen's journey and many adventures, during which he retrieved fire from the belly of a fish, built a *kantele* (a stringed instrument made from the jawbone of a giant pike) and finally departed in his copper boat, predicting he would return to Suomi (the Finnish word for the Finnish nation) to bring new light and songs to the world:

> Suns may rise and set in Suomi,
> Rise and set for generations,
> When the North will learn my teachings,
> Will recall my wisdom-sayings,
> Hungry for the true religion.

> Then will Suomi need my coming,
> Watch for me at dawn of morning,
> That I may bring back the Sampo,
> Bring anew the harp of joyance,
> Bring again the golden moonlight,
> Bring again the silver sunshine,
> Peace and plenty to the Northland.[13]

The Lake Keitele landscapes are among Gallen-Kallela's last, and arguably least literal, painted representations of a *Kalevala* scene. The artist's name and reputation remain as closely associated today with the Finnish national epic as they were in his lifetime. The extent of Gallen-Kallela's contemporary fame, and its indebtedness to his representations of the *Kalevala*, is perhaps best demonstrated by the anecdote of the artist's improbable meeting with the former President of the United States, Theodore Roosevelt, in Nairobi (now in Kenya) in 1909, where they both happened to be staying. 'Good day, Mr Kalevala', said Roosevelt.[14]

The artist's engagement with the *Kalevala* started in the mid-1880s; the great epic and its characters and stories were to provide him with an inexhaustible repertoire of subjects. 'The poems of the *Kalevala* are truly so sacred for me that, for instance, when singing them it feels as if you were resting your weary head upon some strong steadfast support', he confided.[15] His first major work on a *Kalevala* theme was the ambitious *Aino Triptych*, which shows Väinämöinen courting the young Aino, who had been promised to him, but preferred to drown herself in a lake rather than marry the ageing hero (fig. 15). The initial version of the picture, painted in Paris, was exhibited in Helsinki in 1889, publicly linking Gallen-Kallela's name with the *Kalevala* for the first time. When the Finnish Senate commissioned Gallen-Kallela to produce a second version, he decided to give it a greater degree of authenticity. To this end he embarked on a trip to the north-eastern frontier of Finland and to east Karelia, where most of the *Kalevala* songs had originally been collected and where ancient folk poetry and traditions still survived. There the painter found the visual motifs and the ethnographic background he was seeking, intent as he was on 'all [his] Kalevala paintings [being] strictly faithful to nature'.[16]

The *Kalevala*, Gallen-Kallela and Finnish national identity

Many of the ideas and material gathered during that trip were to reach maturation in the next decade, culminating in 1900 with the series of frescoes on themes from the *Kalevala* that Gallen-Kallela painted for the Paris World Fair. Widely praised, this monumental work won the artist international recognition. Set in the Finnish pavilion, which was separate from the Russian section of the Fair, the *Kalevala* frescoes were also intended as a powerful statement of the Finnish national character and patriotism, at a time of growing political tensions. Although part of the Russian Empire, Finland enjoyed a privileged position and retained a degree of autonomy, because it was considered to be a distinct nation. In this context, the *Kalevala*, celebrating Finland's legends and heroic tales, came to embody the idea of a uniquely Finnish heritage, at a moment when Finland was seeking to use its past to construct its modern identity and to justify its calls for political autonomy. Written in Finnish, the *Kalevala* was anchored in the native literary language, thus rehabilitating another crucial element of an independent culture in a nation that had long remained under the influence of Sweden, and where the educated ruling classes still spoke Swedish. 'Finland can [now] say for itself: "I, too, have a history"', exclaimed a contemporary scholar and *Kalevala*-enthusiast.[17] By exalting values of bravery and defiance considered typical of the Finnish spirit, the *Kalevala* became the springboard for nationalist aspirations at a time when Finland was striving for full independence.

The *Kalevala* was fundamentally important for the development of Finnish culture. It offered a wealth of painterly and musical motifs to the artists of the day, not least the composer Jean Sibelius, many of whose musical compositions were based on *Kalevala* themes. Gallen-Kallela and Sibelius enjoyed a rich, creative friendship, and in 1894 Sibelius featured in one of Gallen-Kallela's most ambitious Symbolist works, *Symposium* (1894), about the mystery of artistic creation. As the chief visual interpreter of the *Kalevala* legends, Gallen-Kallela became one of the architects of Finnish national identity and, ultimately, of its independence. Although born, like Sibelius, into a Swedish-speaking family, he made a point of using Finnish,[18] and from 1907 stopped using the Swedish form of his name, Axel Gallén. From this date he systematically signed his works with its Finnicised version, 'Akseli Gallen-Kallela'.[19] Equally

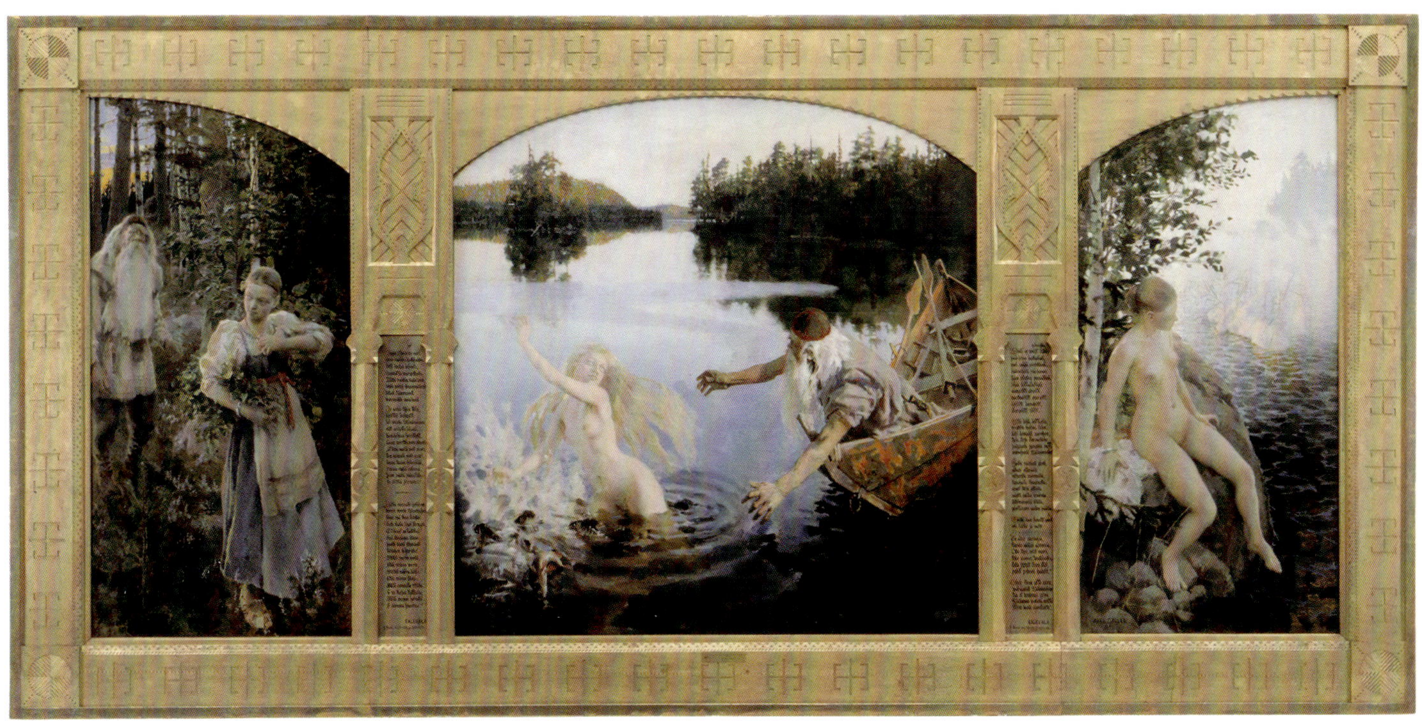

Fig. 15   **Akseli Gallen-Kallela**, *Aino Triptych*, 1891
Oil on canvas, 200 × 413 cm
Finnish National Gallery, Ateneum Art Museum, Helsinki

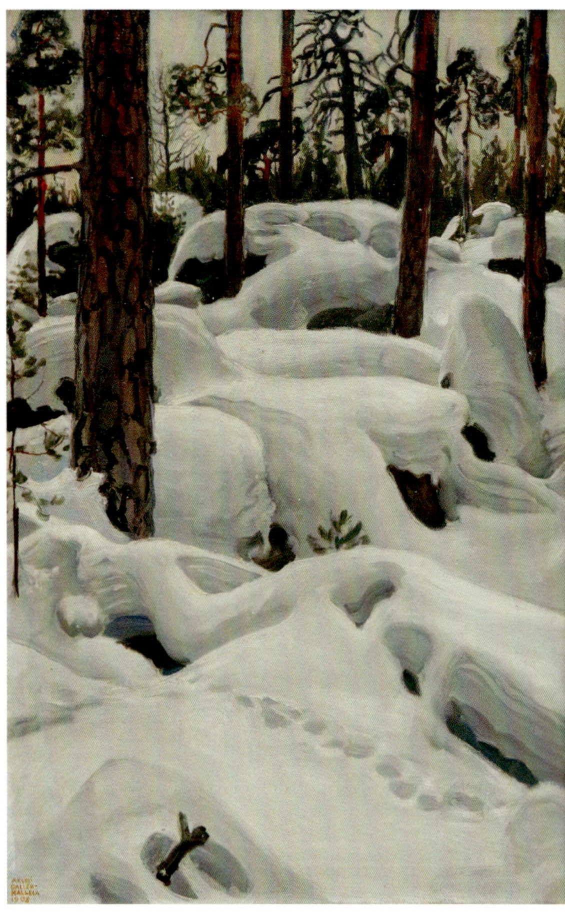

Fig. 16 **Akseli Gallen-Kallela**, *The Den of the Lynx*, 1908
Oil of canvas, 98 × 64 cm
Turku Art Museum

strong patriotic sentiments were promoted in the artistic review *Nuori Suomi*, or *Young Finland*, first published in 1891, with which Sibelius was closely associated. Originally the Christmas supplement of a progressive newspaper, *Päivälehti, Nuori Suomi* hailed the idea of a uniquely Finnish culture. Gallen-Kallela, who was also one of the leading figures of the *Young Finland* circle, fervently embraced the liberation movement. Gallen-Kallela's original, epic narrative style, developed to depict the *Kalevala*, became representative of Finnish nationalism. It stamped itself on Finnish collective identity and bolstered the moves towards independence.

Lake Keitele: a patriotic painting?

In reaction to the national awakening of the 1890s, the Imperial government had reinforced its grip on Finland by imposing measures that intensified the Russification of the country.[20] Such moves provoked the murder of the Russian Governor General of Finland by a nationalist activist on 16 June 1904. Settled at Lintula Villa for the summer, Gallen-Kallela must have been acutely aware of this event. The dramatic news is known to have reached the artist just hours after the incident, by telegram, as he stopped by at the home of his friend Rudolf Ahonius and prompted the two men to celebrate. Consciously or not, Gallen-Kallela may have imbued his images of Lake Keitele, painted that summer, with a political message. During the nineteenth and twentieth centuries many young or emerging nations – including, for instance, the United States, Ireland, Hungary and Czechoslovakia – used landscape as a tool for heralding their identity, glorifying its beauty and vigorous nature as the symbol of their country's many resources and indomitable strength. In the Lake Keitele pictures Gallen-Kallela may have wanted to signal the vital, untamed force of the Finnish lands then threatened by Russian oppression, as indicated by the frieze of heavy clouds hovering above the lake. In others of his works, the Imperial Russian presence is symbolised by a heavy coat of snow smothering the land, desperate to be freed from the Russian yoke (fig. 16).

Whatever role – directly or indirectly – Gallen-Kallela's paintings might have played in Finland's long struggle to become a nation, the artist was certainly instrumental in constructing Finland's official image during the process of building its political identity.

Finland finally achieved independence from Russia in December 1917, following the February and October Revolutions and the fall of Tsar Nicholas II, when the Communist leader Vladimir Lenin accepted its 'free detachment' from the Russian Empire.

Gallen-Kallela's highly original pictures on themes from the *Kalevala* helped to elaborate a new Finnish national style, as did what could be called his 'ideological' landscapes. The Lake Keitele pictures – pure landscapes, but directly inspired by the *Kalevala* – belong to the genres of both mythology and landscape, and in that sense may be counted among his most patriotic works, even though they were painted during the last years of the artist's so-called 'heroic' *Kalevala* period. Gallen-Kallela's direct political engagement resumed in 1918 when a civil war erupted between the Finnish Communists, acting under orders from Lenin, and the Whites, supported by Germany and Marshall Mannerheim, General of the Finnish Army. Serving as Mannerheim's aide-de-camp, Gallen-Kallela further asserted his role as Finland's 'national artist', this time as the official purveyor of designs for symbols of the new Finnish state, including medals, insignia, uniforms, flags and banknotes.

Long before this date, however, Gallen-Kallela had achieved social respectability in Finland, and beyond. In 1914, like many successful painters before him (such as Rembrandt, Rubens, Velázquez, Ingres and Corot), he was commissioned by the Uffizi Gallery in Florence to make a self portrait for its unique collection of artists' self portraits, and at his death in 1931 he was given a state funeral (fig. 17). By the final years of his life Gallen-Kallela had become a staunchly conservative figure. Although a similar trajectory was shared by a number of early twentieth-century painters, particularly those associated with nationalist movements, it is hard to reconcile this with our perception of the cosmopolitan and innovative young Axel Gallén. This further complicates any assessment of the Lake Keitele pictures as Modernist masterpieces (a notion that in any case requires caution, as Modernism in Nordic painting at the end of the nineteenth century and the beginning of the twentieth did not develop in parallel with the European avant-garde, but followed its own stylistic evolution).[21]

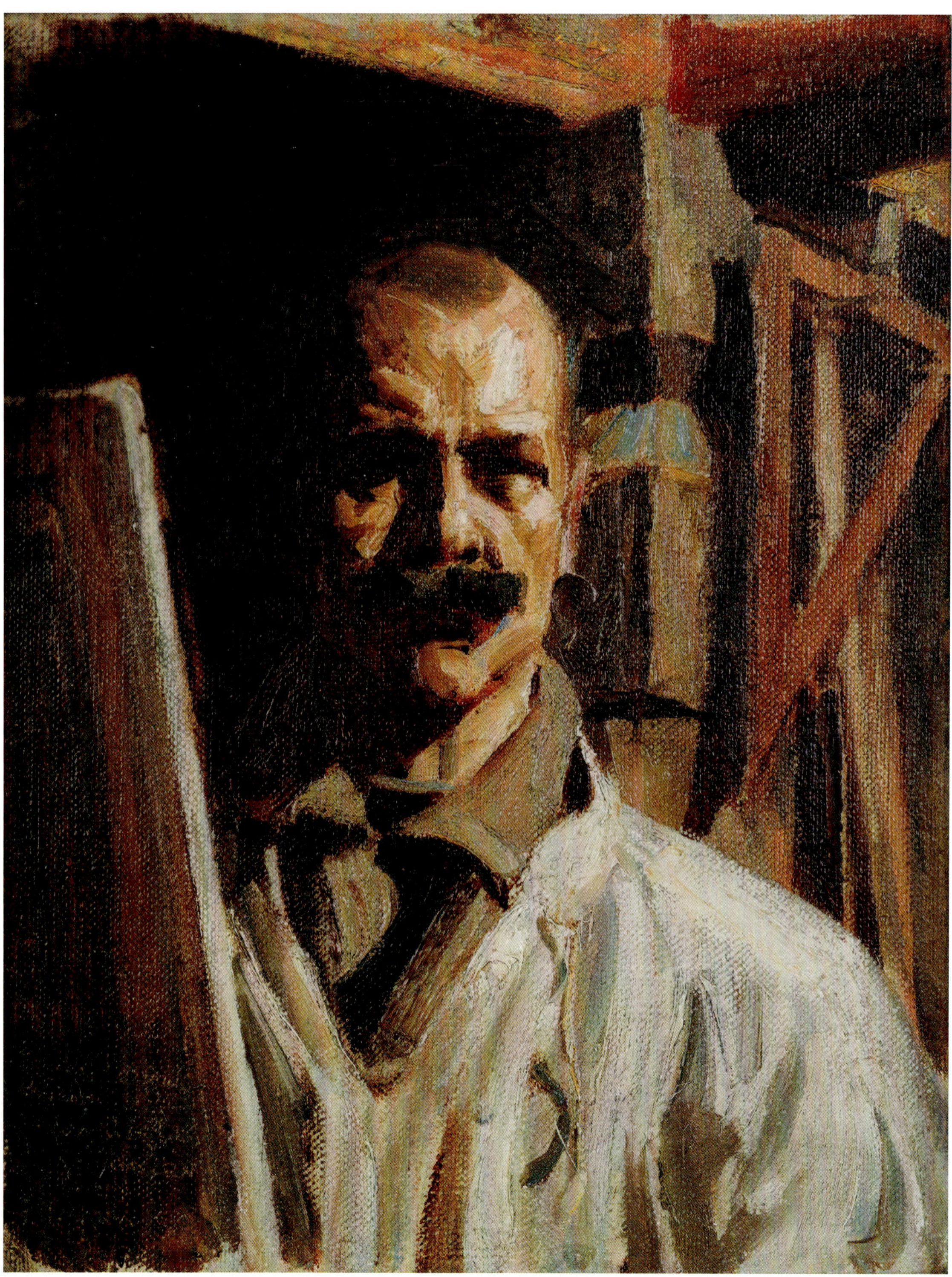

Fig. 17 **Akseli Gallen-Kallela**, *Self Portrait for the Uffizi,
Florence*, 1916
Oil on canvas, 50 × 39.5 cm
Gallen-Kallela Museum, Espoo

Lake Keitele: a radical work by an avant-garde artist?

From the early 1890s Gallen-Kallela's career had gained momentum through regular exhibitions of his work in the main European cities. These exhibitions brought him into contact with radical artists, and demonstrated that he was to be considered among the most advanced and inspiring artists internationally. A short while after his first show in Berlin at Galerie Gurlitt on Potsdamer Strasse in early 1895, Gallen-Kallela held a joint exhibition in the same city with Edvard Munch, which generated fruitful exchanges between the men; Gallen-Kallela was impressed by Munch's bold Symbolist compositions.[22] Further encounters with German and Polish intellectuals and artists, painters and engravers, often held at the restaurant Zum Schwartzen Ferkel, resulted in Gallen-Kallela's collaboration with the new art periodical *Pan*, based in Berlin. Having started to make prints just a few months earlier, Gallen-Kallela was invited to join *Pan*'s editorial board and to produce engravings for the magazine.

In the early twentieth century the naive simplicity of Gallen-Kallela's works attracted the interest of the newest generation of artists working in Germany, such as Wassily Kandinsky, who in 1902 invited him to take part in the fourth exhibition of his *Phalanx* group in Munich. Three years later Gallen-Kallela crossed paths with another newly founded German avant-garde group, Die Brücke. Its members, notably Erich Heckel, were intrigued by an exhibition of Gallen-Kallela's prints at the Emil Richter Gallery in Dresden. By then the Finnish artist had started to garner honours; his work had been the subject of a monographic study published in 1904,[23] and individual paintings were entering the collections of museums and galleries in Eastern Europe where his work fascinated the boldest young artists.[24] After a successful trip to Hungary in 1907, when his *Young Faun* was purchased by the Budapest Art Museum (fig. 18), Gallen-Kallela was invited to become a member of Die Brücke, and showed a selection of his works, including a number of woodcuts, in the group's second exhibition in Dresden.

The Die Brücke artists shared with Gallen-Kallela a desire to emphasise intuition, sensation and subjective feelings in their art, neglecting traditional rules of perspective and academic proportions in favour of a heightened sense of immediacy, enhanced in their paintings by impulsive, high-keyed, non-naturalistic colours.

Fig. 18　**Akseli Gallen-Kallela**, *Young Faun*, 1904
Oil on canvas, 67 × 65 cm
Museum of Fine Arts, Budapest

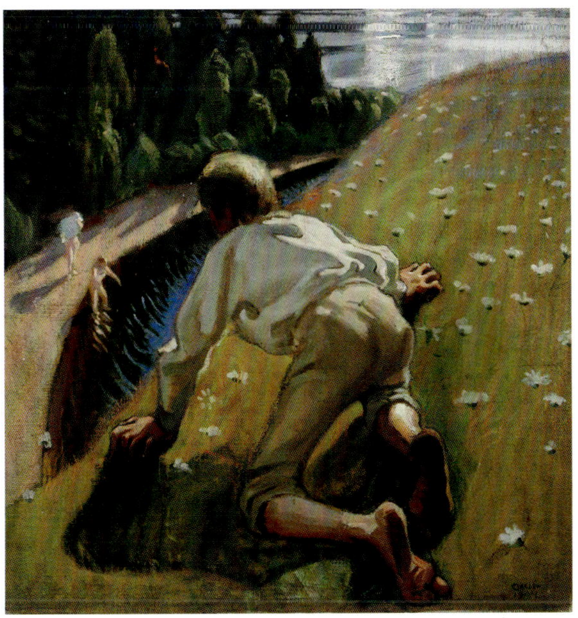

They also strove to position themselves on the international art scene: this may have played a part in their approaching Gallen-Kallela, whose reputation was firmly established. However, their collaboration was short-lived. When invited to contribute a print to the Die Brücke portfolio in 1908, Gallen-Kallela sent a woodcut made 13 years earlier – *Flower of Death* – rather than a new creation. This went against the rules set by the group and precipitated the end of their joint venture. Like many other experimental movements in the early twentieth century, Die Brücke turned to Africa for inspiration. So, of course, did Gallen-Kallela. However, his 1909 trip to East Africa was unconnected to the German artists' interest in so-called 'primitivist art'. By then he was losing contact with Die Brücke, and his expedition failed to reinforce his link with the group.

Gallen-Kallela and modern art

Gallen-Kallela's multifaceted personality, the fact that he created art that was at once traditional and innovative, and his experimentation with a variety of techniques, make him and his work difficult to categorise. To an extent the Realist and Symbolist styles that he adopted during and following his Paris years were already outdated when he came to embrace them. Quick-tempered and caustic, at times tempestuous, he swiftly dismissed the ideas and goals of much contemporary art: Impressionist pictures were deemed 'bloody, dastardly deed[s]'.[25] He did not share the Impressionist painters' obsession with capturing the changes of light in individual paintings, or making series of canvases displaying the same place or motif at different times of the day. Unlike Monet's 'series paintings', which were intended to be exhibited together, Gallen-Kallela's four Lake Keitele landscapes appear never to have been shown side by side in the artist's lifetime. The four versions of Lake Keitele differ from one another in mood and atmosphere, and each depicts the lake with various degrees of faithfulness to nature. Also unlike Monet, Gallen-Kallela did not set out to record the variations of weather or atmosphere in a single artistic project where each picture forms one element of a whole; instead, the Lake Keitele landscapes evolved from empirical observation to a greater degree of stylisation, with an increasing emphasis on mythical content (cat 11).

Implacable in his judgement of Impressionism, Gallen-Kallela showed no more mercy for the art of the Fauves, even though his *Oceanides*, painted in Paris in 1909, just before his departure to Africa, share some similarities with André Derain's and Matisse's bold, sensual dancers and bathers set in Arcadian landscapes.[26] Gallen-Kallela's description of his encounter with the pioneer Parisian art dealer Ambroise Vollard in the same year gives a sense of his unwillingness to acknowledge developments in modern art:

> Yesterday I had breakfast with an art dealer [Vollard]. We sat in his cellar eating and telling sailor jokes and before I left he showed me his Gauguins. That fellow Gauguin has driven everyone quite mad. They gape blankly at his art without the slightest glimmer of understanding, but follow him like sheep all the same. There are hundreds of these parrots, all equally dreadful [...] Nowadays you can paint however you please, as long as you stick to the colours that are in fashion. Today's artists see the world as nothing but confetti, a jumping, screaming, shapeless abyss. When I was a young lad, this was the kind of rubbish we painted in secret up in the attic. Forget the human anatomy, the body must be distorted beyond all recognition.[27]

The attraction of distant lands

Gallen-Kallela's reluctance to embrace the most modern artistic trends he had encountered in Paris may have led him to escape to East Africa. He felt excitement and a renewed sense of power when faced with the untouched, dazzling landscapes of Kenya, resplendent under the intense, glaring African sun. Installed with his family near Nairobi, he studied native life, local flora and fauna, and, as in Karelia almost 20 years earlier, he collected specimens and artefacts for the ethnographic collection he was building. Gallen-Kallela painted about 150 pictures in Africa, often small and swiftly executed studies of unspoiled lakes and rivers, which he observed in the same way as he did the landscapes of his beloved Finland (fig. 19).

Gallen-Kallela felt the need to reconnect with the people and the natural environment that had captivated him on his search for 'real' *Kalevala* types in Karelia. Before departing for Africa, he was

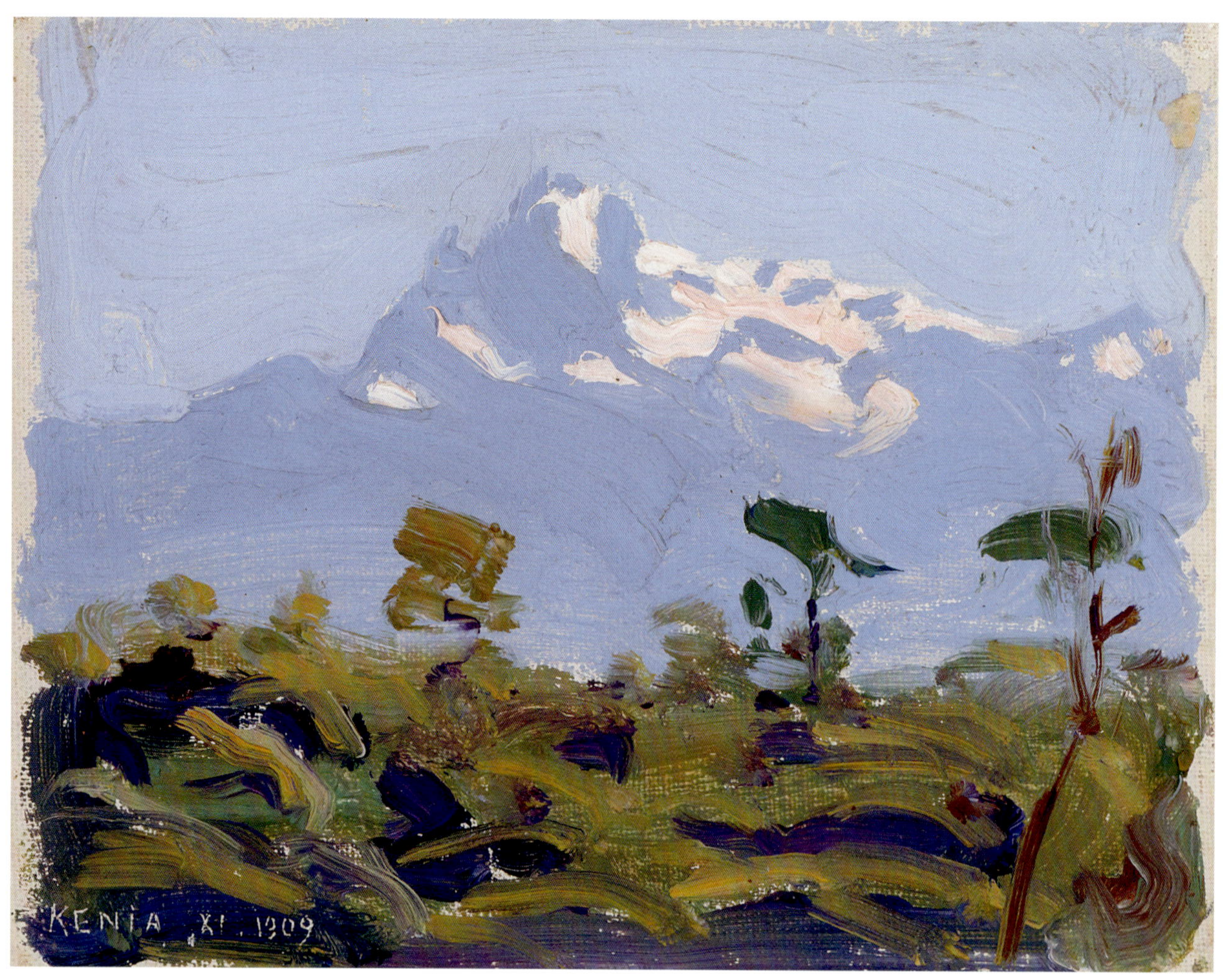

Fig. 19   **Akseli Gallen-Kallela**, *Mount Kenya*, 1909–10
Oil on panel, 13 × 17 cm
Finnish National Gallery, Ateneum Art Museum, Helsinki

hoping that there would be '[there] a branch of the Kalevala people, even though it's already extinct in Finland!'[28] It is likely that the same urge took him to New Mexico in the mid-1920s, during a trip to the USA. On this occasion he visited the remote artists' colony of Taos, far from modern urban civilisation. The need for isolation and immersion in the raw beauty of distant lands allowed him to widen his horizons. Just as Gallen-Kallela had earlier experienced in the remote Finnish countryside, his senses were again reawakened through his removal from civilisation. Ironically, for this avowedly anti-Modernist artist, such a conscious departure from the 'civilised' world was in itself a central trend in Modernism. Gauguin, whose art was derided by Gallen-Kallela, had escaped contemporary society in a similar self-imposed exile from the modern world.

Lake Keitele: A modern ode to nature

Whatever Gallen-Kallela's place in the history of the avant-gardes, his views of Lake Keitele may be the artist's greatest contribution to the grammar of national and international Modernism. Gallen-Kallela stands out as the major representative of cosmopolitan culture and Finnish identity in art, yet he remains much more than a merely Finnish or nationalist painter; he was also an inspired observer of his country's natural beauty. His Lake Keitele paintings represent perhaps his most sensitive ode to nature: 'Art is an immense, eternal forest [...]', he wrote. 'The moon, sun and all kind of glittering stars move about at your will, and when you want to come to the shore of a lake in the wilderness it is fathomless if you so want'.[29]

Catalogue

Akseli Gallen-Kallela
Boats on the Shore, 1884

Oil on canvas, attached on hardboard, 31.5 × 40 cm
Finnish National Gallery, Ateneum Art Museum,
Helsinki, Finland, Antell Collections

Painted when the artist was barely 20, *Boats on the Shore* attests to Gallen-Kallela's profound affinity with the Finnish countryside. Growing up in Tyrvää, in rural western Finland, he had developed a deep, sensory familiarity with the natural environment. 'If I want to feel as one with nature, I need to walk in bare feet – the sole of the foot starts to engage with the nuances of the earth', he declared.[1] The trees, lakes and inhabitants of Tyrvää, where his father was the local chief of police, provided him with his first subjects to paint. His early animal studies and sensitive, unpretentious landscapes express his empathy with nature. Here, the clear, gently agitated water of a lake, its rocky shore and beached boats, a wooded island and remote forest, are scrutinised under his brush, their textures truthfully rendered and translated with differentiated strokes of paint. These show the artist's precocious skill at evoking the simple, quiet beauty of the landscape, using a technique based on direct observation. Produced a few months before he was to travel to Paris on a bursary from the Finnish Senate, Gallen-Kallela was already aware of contemporary currents in French painting: his dry, muted style alludes to the works of painter Jules Bastien-Lepage (1848–1884) and his doctrine of plein-air realism, which exerted a considerable influence on Nordic painters. Albert Edelfelt (1854–1905), Gallen-Kallela's great friend and mentor, owned reproductions of Bastien-Lepage's paintings, which left a lasting impression on the young artist, impressed by the French painter's precise touch and the modest, noble banality of his rural scenes. Yet in *Boats on the Shore* Gallen-Kallela is already imposing his own style and the originality of his vision. The boats depicted, in all their ordinariness, are charged with meaning, suggesting the embarkations by the heroes of the national epic *Kalevala*. Their adventures – with which the painter had been deeply familiar since childhood, when bards would come and sing *Kalevala* poems in his family home – were set in such raw, untouched landscapes. With its diagonal structure, and its allusion to Finland's heroic tales, *Boats on the Shore* looks forward to the artist's most coherent and complex works, not least his Lake Keitele landscapes.

1 Paris 1998, p. 36.

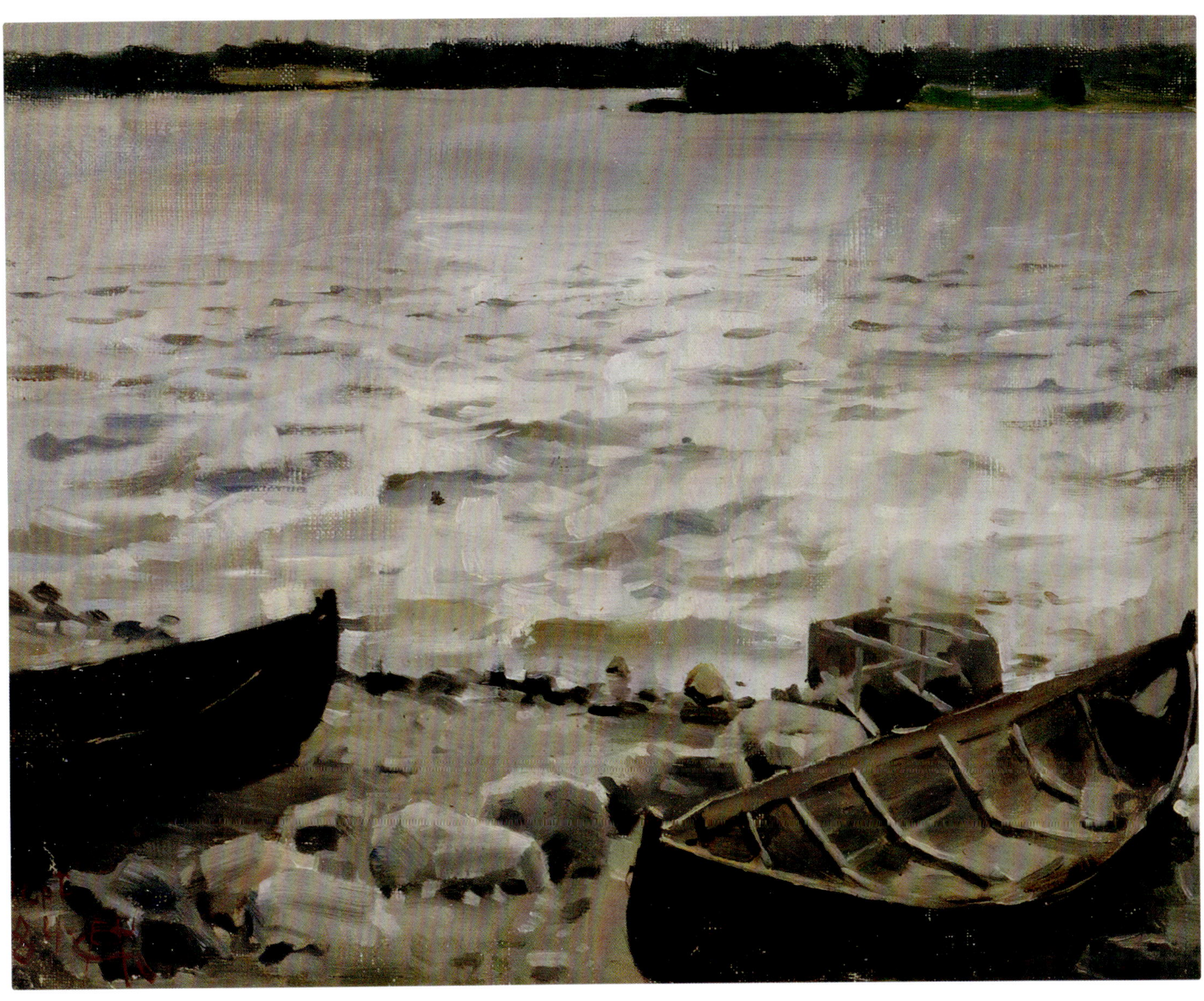

Cat. 2

Akseli Gallen-Kallela
Rouse Thyself Finland!, 1896

Stained glass, 26 × 37 cm
Gallen-Kallela Museum, Espoo, Finland

Fig. 20   Stained-glass panel, English, about 1537
Clear and coloured glass, leaded, with painted and
stained decoration
Victoria and Albert Museum (C.456-1919)

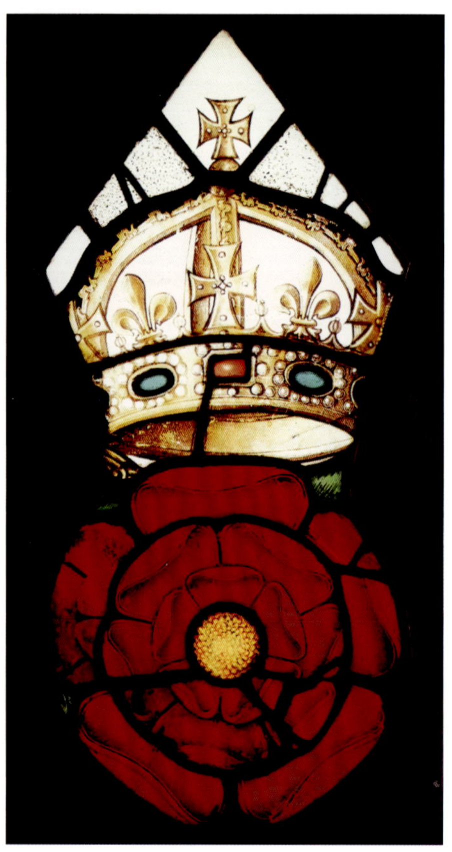

An eminently versatile and multifaceted artist, Gallen-Kallela
worked in a variety of media and showed great dexterity in his
practice of traditional crafts. His interest in the applied arts culminated in the mid-1890s with the design and construction of his
house, a 'wilderness studio' called Kalela. A trip to London in 1895,
as the house was being built, drew his attention to the English Arts
and Crafts movement, which blurred the boundaries between crafts
and the fine arts.[1] In London he acquired a printing press on which
he experimented with printmaking, and a glass furnace for glass-
staining, widening his skills and broadening his horizons. This
stained glass was one of the first of very few pieces that Gallen-
Kallela realised in his fully equipped Kalela studio, marking the start
of a new creative period.[2] It was not only the furnace, but also the
motif itself that came from London: the artist and his wife had
visited the South Kensington Museum (now the Victoria and Albert
Museum) where he copied, in his sketchbook, a sixteenth-century
stained-glass panel of a Lancastrian rose, then on long-term loan
to the museum (fig. 20).[3] Gallen-Kallela's drawing formed the basis
for his own stained-glass work, in which Finland's heraldic white
rose rises behind a lakeside landscape, typical of the Finnish
countryside. These elements are here turned into emblems of the
country's cultural nationalism, at a time when relations between
Russia and the Grand Duchy of Finland were becoming strained.
This stained-glass piece may look like a religious artwork, yet its
message is entirely political. Its title, *Rouse Thyself Finland!*, comes
from a choral song composed in 1882 by Emil Genetz to celebrate
the eightieth birthday of the writer Elias Lönnrot, the influential
compiler of the *Kalevala* in the 1830s.[4] Glorifying Finnish legends,
culture and language, this patriotic song came to embody the
struggle against an ever-tighter Russian oppression, during a period
when Finland was gaining a greater sense of its own identity.
A rallying cry, it would later provide the basis for the hymn theme
in *Finlandia*, the equally politically charged symphonic poem by
Jean Sibelius, a close friend of Gallen-Kallela, who sat for the
artist on several occasions. Here the lakeside landscape, a motif
recurrent in the painter's oeuvre, is imbued with patriotic feelings,
emphasising the heroic roots of the nation.

1   Gallen-Kallela-Sirén 2005, p. 136.
2   Helsinki 1996, pp. 314–15.
3   We are grateful to Minna Turtiainen, Collections Manager, at the Gallen-Kallela
    Museum, Espoo, for generously sharing this information with us.
4   Strasbourg 1999, pp. 167–9.

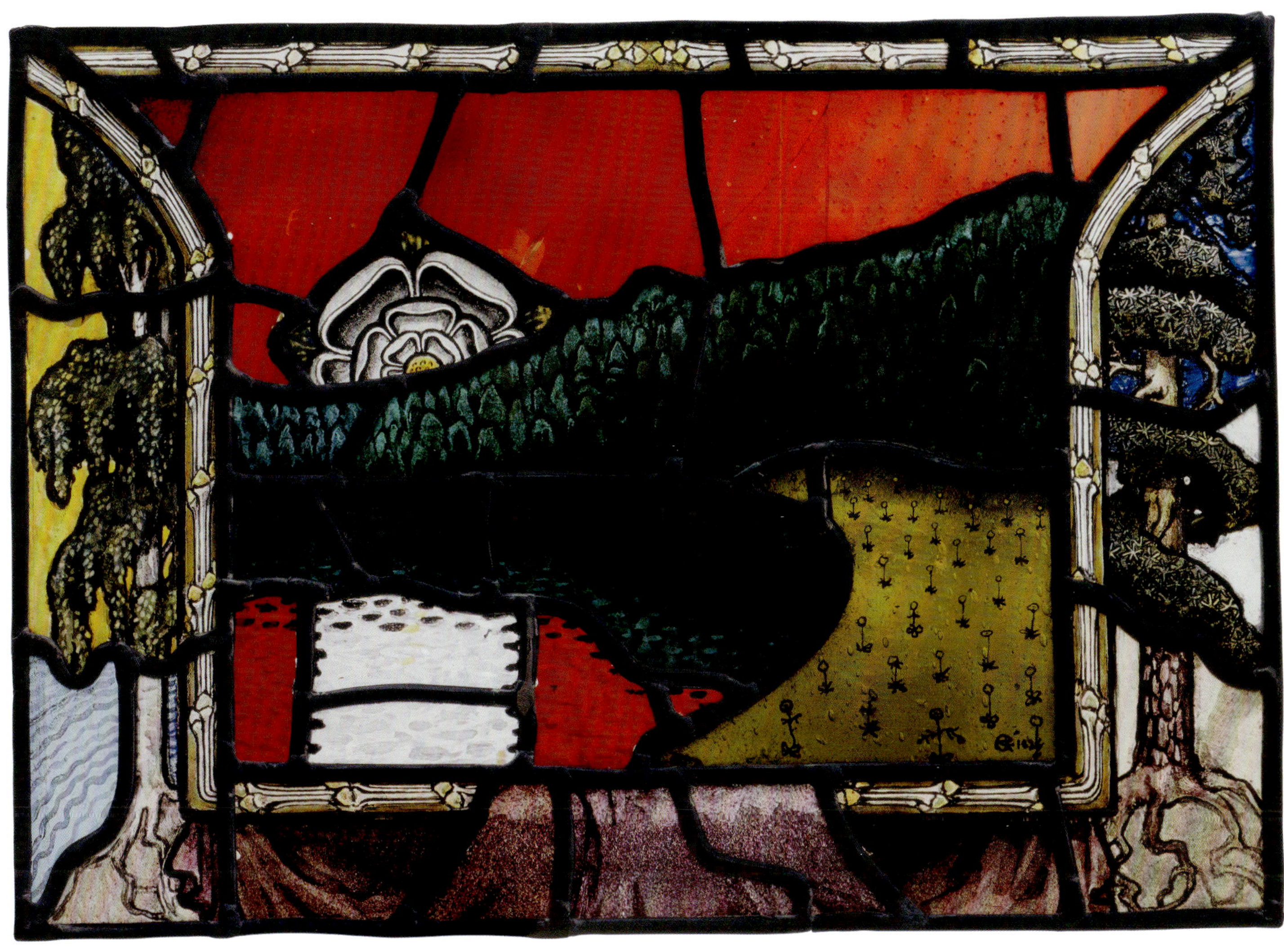

Cat. 3

Akseli Gallen-Kallela
Lake View, 1901

Oil on canvas, 84 × 57 cm
Finnish National Gallery, Ateneum Art Museum,
Helsinki, Finland

Fig. 21 **Albert Edelfelt**, *Kaukola Ridge at Sunset*, 1889–90
Oil on canvas, 116.5 × 83 cm
Finnish National Gallery, Ateneum Art Museum, Helsinki

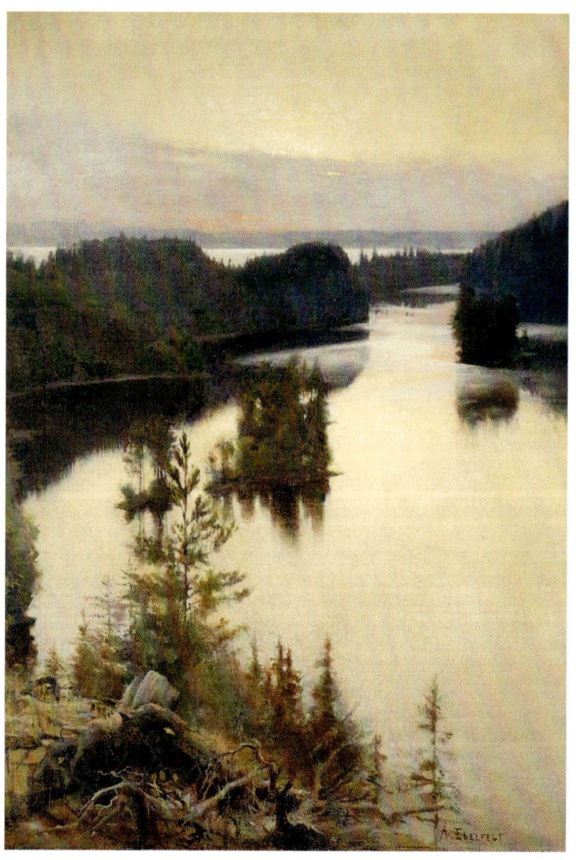

By 1901 Gallen-Kallela was exhibiting widely in the capital cities of Europe and completing official commissions for major, large-scale decorative projects, which involved long periods of travel abroad. Yet he felt the call of his homeland and was most at ease in the pure, unspoilt wilderness of his native country. 'While in my soul shine attractive images of distant countries, from my inner self arises another image, quiet and familiar: the solitude of an untouched forest. A marsh surrounded by moss and lakeside plants [...] A migrating hawk shrieks in the evening's transparent air', he wrote.[1] Yearning for the backwoods and deep countryside of Finland, the artist regularly returned to Kalela, his log studio house where he realised some of his greatest *Kalevala* paintings, in a new, vigorous and archaic visual language. Built on Pöytäniemi headland, which dominates Lake Ruovesi, the house was large and impressive; it was planned to the very last detail by Gallen-Kallela himself, inspired by the imposing farmhouses of Karelia, in eastern Finland, where he had spent his honeymoon. It was also genuinely isolated by both forest and water, and usually accessible only by boat, or just by skis in winter. He lived there as a recluse, enjoying the solitude and finding refuge in the middle of nature. This painting invites us to share his primitive joy at being immersed in the landscape. Realistically observed branches in the foreground – the tips of plants or trees – help establish the scale of the natural site, positioning us in it, as Gallen-Kallela embraced this view probably from Kalela itself. A superb scene unfolds: he has masterfully conveyed the dramatic effect of light piercing through the sky, and the silvery bar cutting across the lake's sheen anticipates the arresting depictions of Lake Keitele that he was to paint a few years later. The artist had experimented with vertical landscapes – a format not normally used for this genre – in the early 1890s in Symbolist paintings of lakes and forests (fig. 10). He was also no doubt influenced by Albert Edelfelt's spectacular *Kaukola Ridge at Sunset* (fig. 21). The verticality of *Lake View* dramatically emphasises the depth of the site, a trick Edelfeldt and Gallen-Kallela may have learnt from looking at Japanese prints. Bathed in the hazy evening light of the Nordic summer, *Lake View* exudes a sense of plein-air naturalism, while conveying a world of dreams and of an impossibly fresh and virginal nature.

1 Gallen-Kallela 1955, p. 83.

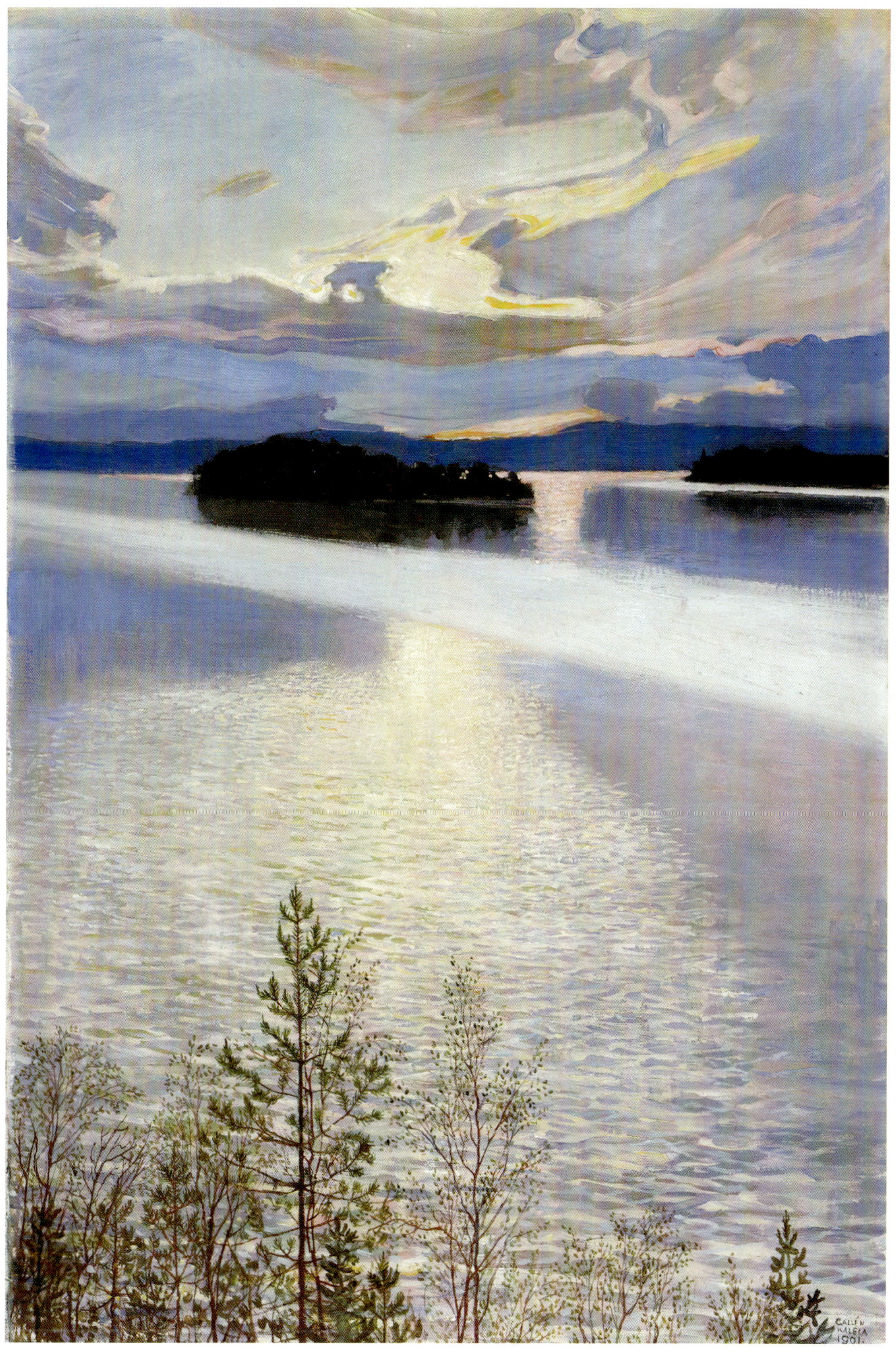

Akseli Gallen-Kallela
Mary Gallén on the Lakeshore at Lintula,
1904

Oil on canvas, 24 × 33 cm
Private collection; on deposit in the Gallen-Kallela
Museum, Espoo, Finland

Painted in 1904, this portrait shows Mary Gallén, the artist's wife, posing on the shore by Lintula Villa, in central Finland: a lakeside lodge Gallen-Kallela had rented for the summer months. He had been travelling for the early part of that year, first to Vienna where he had shown works at the Vienna Secession exhibition; then, with his wife, to northern Italy, the south of France and Spain, where he contracted malaria. By the time the couple returned to Finland in May, he had still not recovered and Lintula Villa, near Konginkangas, proved better suited, and more accessible, for the convalescing painter, than the large, impractical and isolated Kalela. The house overlooked Lake Keitele, whose placid waters were a soothing sight for Gallen-Kallela: he made them the background of this small, spontaneous portrait of his wife. A talented musician, the mother of his children and his most trusted companion, Mary was also Gallen-Kallela's favourite model. To enhance her features he often posed her, and his other sitters – generally relatives or dear friends – in front of a decorative backdrop: a traditional rug, an ornamental frieze of stylised Art Nouveau motifs or a rocky setting.[1] Here Mary's face is delicately delineated against the landscape's near-abstract pattern, much like that of her sister Anna, who sat for the *Spring* fresco in the artist's recently completed Jusélius mausoleum, where a young woman stands out against a lake background (fig. 5). However, the simplicity of this portrait links it most strongly to Gallen-Kallela's folk portraits of the late 1880s. Its swift execution contributes to the work's overall informality: its main elements are sketched out with quick strokes, while scratches into the paint, done with the end of the brush, depict the tall reeds by the shore. Mary's pose entirely lacks affectation: placed off-centre, in a thoughtful, serene attitude, she turns back as if her attention had suddenly been caught; the close bond between painter and sitter is palpable. Above all, the painting is a celebration of the return to a quiet life, good health and the delectable few months of glorious Finnish summer.

1 *Portrait of the Artist's Wife*, 1893, Ateneum, in Helsinki 1996, p. 132.

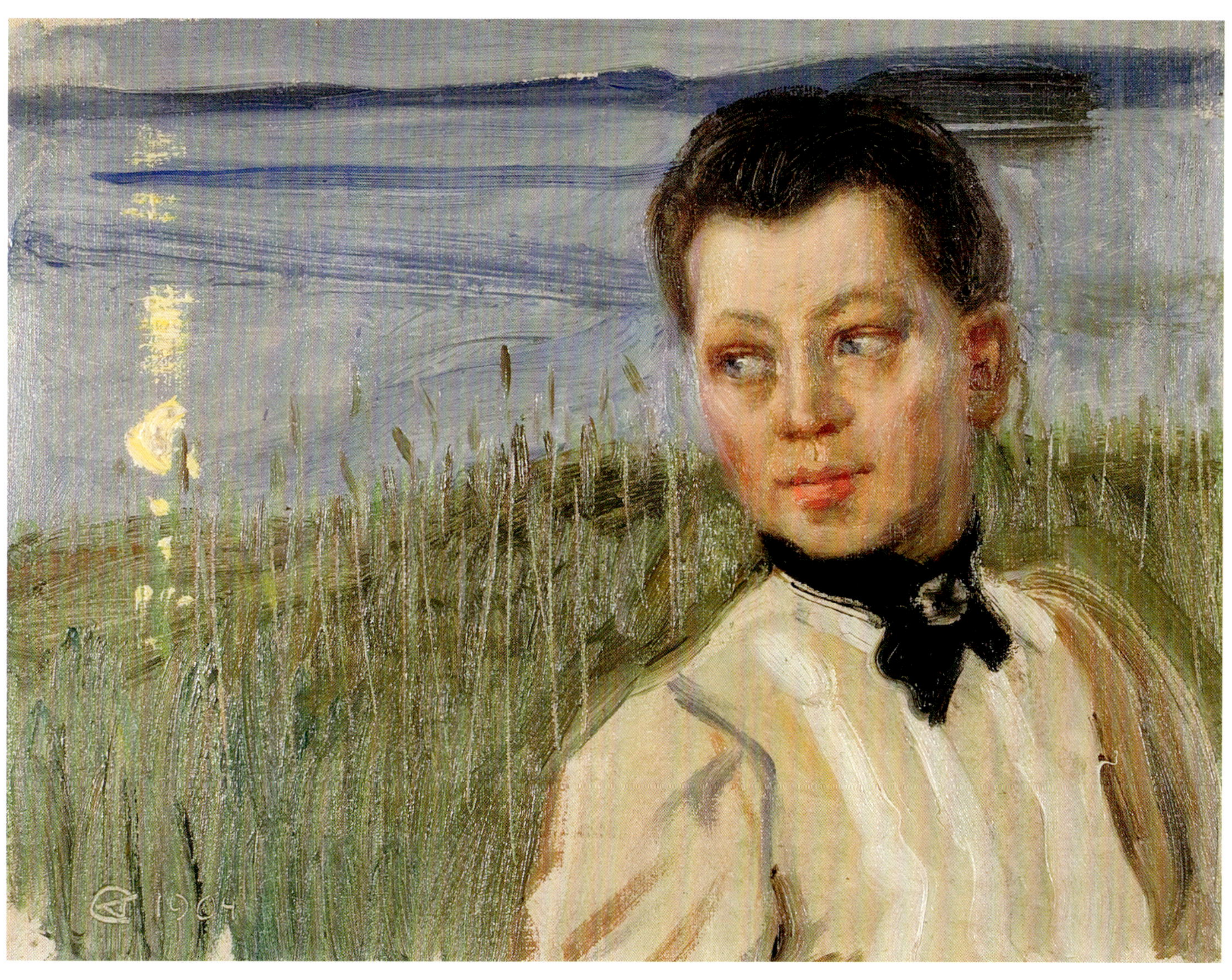

Cat. 5

Akseli Gallen-Kallela
Lake Keitele, 1904

Oil on canvas, 50 × 65 cm
Private collection; on deposit in the Gallen-Kallela
Museum, Espoo, Finland

As evidenced by the portrait of Mary on the lakeshore at Lintula (cat. 4), which is likely to have been painted on the spot, some of Gallen-Kallela's views of Lake Keitele originate from direct observation. Yet this painting, probably the first of his several versions of this composition, shows the artist moving away from the naturalism of the portrait of his wife. In this landscape, larger and less anecdotal, Lake Keitele becomes the single motif and the sole object of the painter's fascination. The landscape is allowed to expand in all its glory, deploying itself like a panorama, energised by the linear patterns of the wind on the water. In this version, Gallen-Kallela's recent work for the Jusélius mausoleum – six frescoes on the themes of life, death and renewal, which were completed the previous summer – is clear (fig. 5), its impact apparent in the diagonal lines animating the picture, bordered by hard black outlines. These isolate the various elements of the landscape, but also recall the strongly marked contours and simplified shapes of the artist's great *Kalevala* scenes painted in the previous decade. This severe, firm-lined decorative style formed part of Gallen-Kallela's cultivated archaism. It originated in his interest in, and realisation of, stained-glass works, made of clear fields of colour separated by thick black contours. The painting also bears the mark of textile works: traditional Karelian rug ornamentation was based on simple linear and angular motifs, and Gallen-Kallela's own textiles, influenced by folklore and ethnography, showed similar patterns. Here, the gridded composition of intersecting lines evokes woven textiles, and lends the painting a flat, ornamental appearance. The dark trees massed on the distant island of Haapasaari also echo the flames, or fern-like shapes, of the artist's 'Flame' rug, his best-known work in that field (fig. 4). Executed with an assured hand and a confident brush, the painting exudes a unique intensity and primitive vigour. It remained with the artist until his death in 1931, and was shown in the memorial exhibition organised in his honour in Helsinki four years later.[1]

1 *Akseli Gallen-Kallela Memorial Exhibition – 100th Anniversary of the Kalevala*, Helsinki Exhibition Hall, 28 February–17 March 1935, no. 350. Cats 4 and 6 were also included in the exhibition, as nos 301 and 328 respectively.

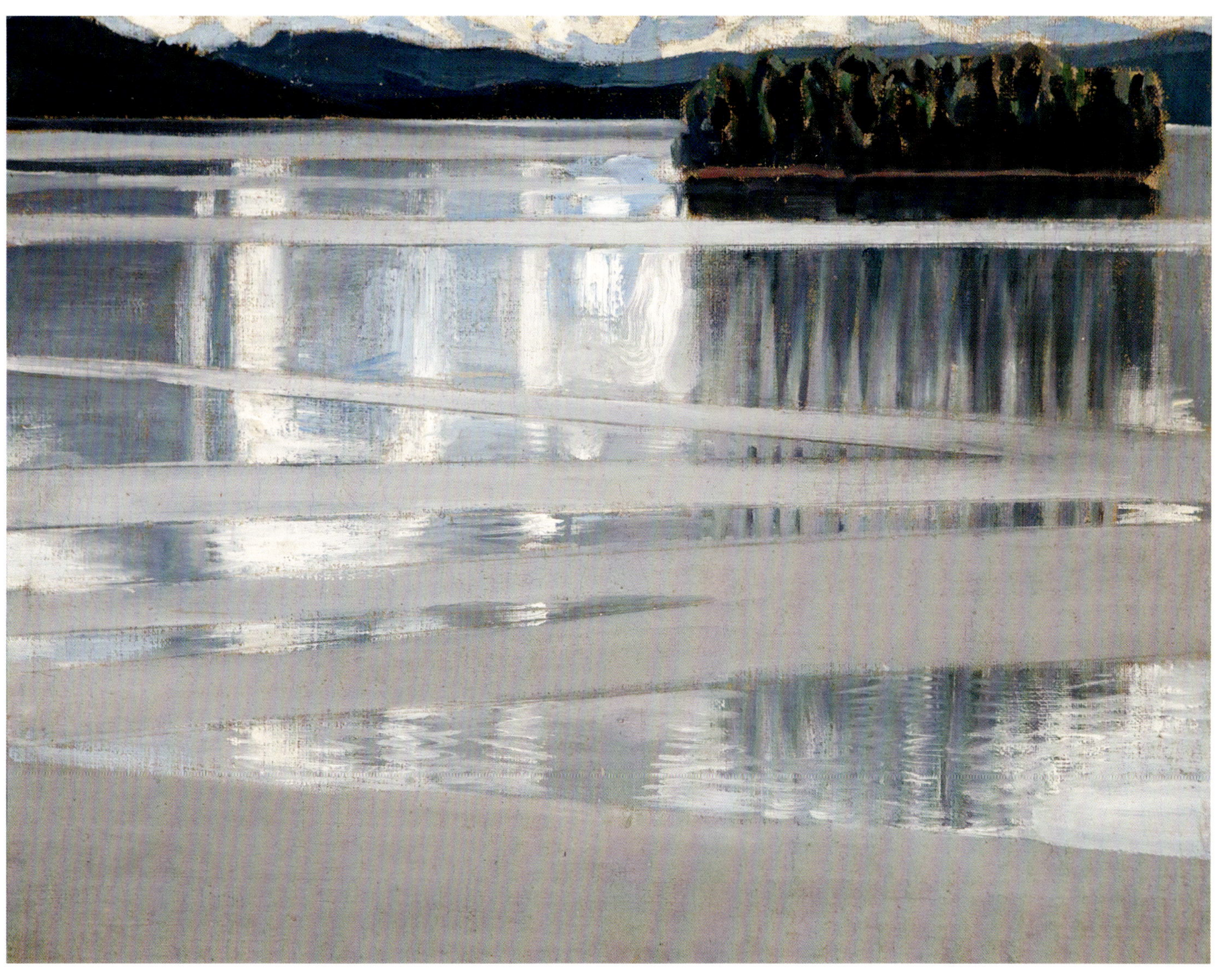

Cat. 6

Akseli Gallen-Kallela
Lake Keitele, 1905

Oil on canvas, 53 × 67 cm
Lahti Art Museum/Viipuri Foundation

Dated 1905, this view of Lake Keitele repeats with minor variations the composition of the painting on deposit in the Gallen-Kallela Museum (cat. 5), presumably executed in 1904 while at Lintula Villa. This work, one of four parallel versions of the Lake Keitele landscape, displays similar characteristics to the latter: a simplification of the elements of the landscape, an emphasis on the decorative and a synthesis between observed reality and stylisation of the motif. Throughout his long career, Gallen-Kallela was no stranger to the idea of repeating his compositions, which in some cases exist in a number of versions. He would occasionally treat the same theme or motif in a variety of media: for example, his *The Defense of the Sampo* (1896), a major composition on a *Kalevala* theme, which he executed as a wooden relief, a woodcut, a tempera painting and a fresco on one of the cupolas of the Paris World Fair's Finnish Pavilion. Gallen-Kallela would also sketch or paint the same motif studied from various points of view, or in different weather conditions, yet without intending each picture as one part of a whole, unlike Claude Monet and his series paintings. Most often Gallen-Kallela would repeat a subject for entirely pragmatic reasons: when a buyer had been found for a work, but the artist was too attached to part with it; or when his works sold and more buyers expressed interest in the same pieces. For an artist who worked so extensively in the field of graphic design and the applied arts, the notion of an artwork's uniqueness probably had little relevance. Yet the Lake Keitele landscapes stand out in Gallen-Kallela's production, as reiterations of the same composition with only minor formal stylistic variations. The integrity and particular harmony of this landscape may have incited him to paint a new version in the months following the completion of what seems to be the initial picture. As in the latter, a large, flat area of pure grey colour covers about one quarter of the canvas's surface, rising up to the top of the lake in a dynamic, rhythmical zigzag. Bathed in acute sunlight, the painting is shot through with jewel-like brilliance. Its metallic, silvery tones (not unlike the atmosphere of Albert Edelfelt's highly influential *A Child's Funeral* of 1879, a bright plein-air painting, that Gallen-Kallela knew well) ooze a particular radiance. Reflections glitter above the lake; the mood is tranquil and ethereal, like in a timeless Arcadia. This painting, exhibited in 1906 in a show organised in Vyborg (Viipuri in Finnish) by the city's Art Lovers Association, was purchased in the same year by the city council.[1]

1 Exhibition of Vyborg Art Lovers Association, 4 February–4 March 1906, no. 37.

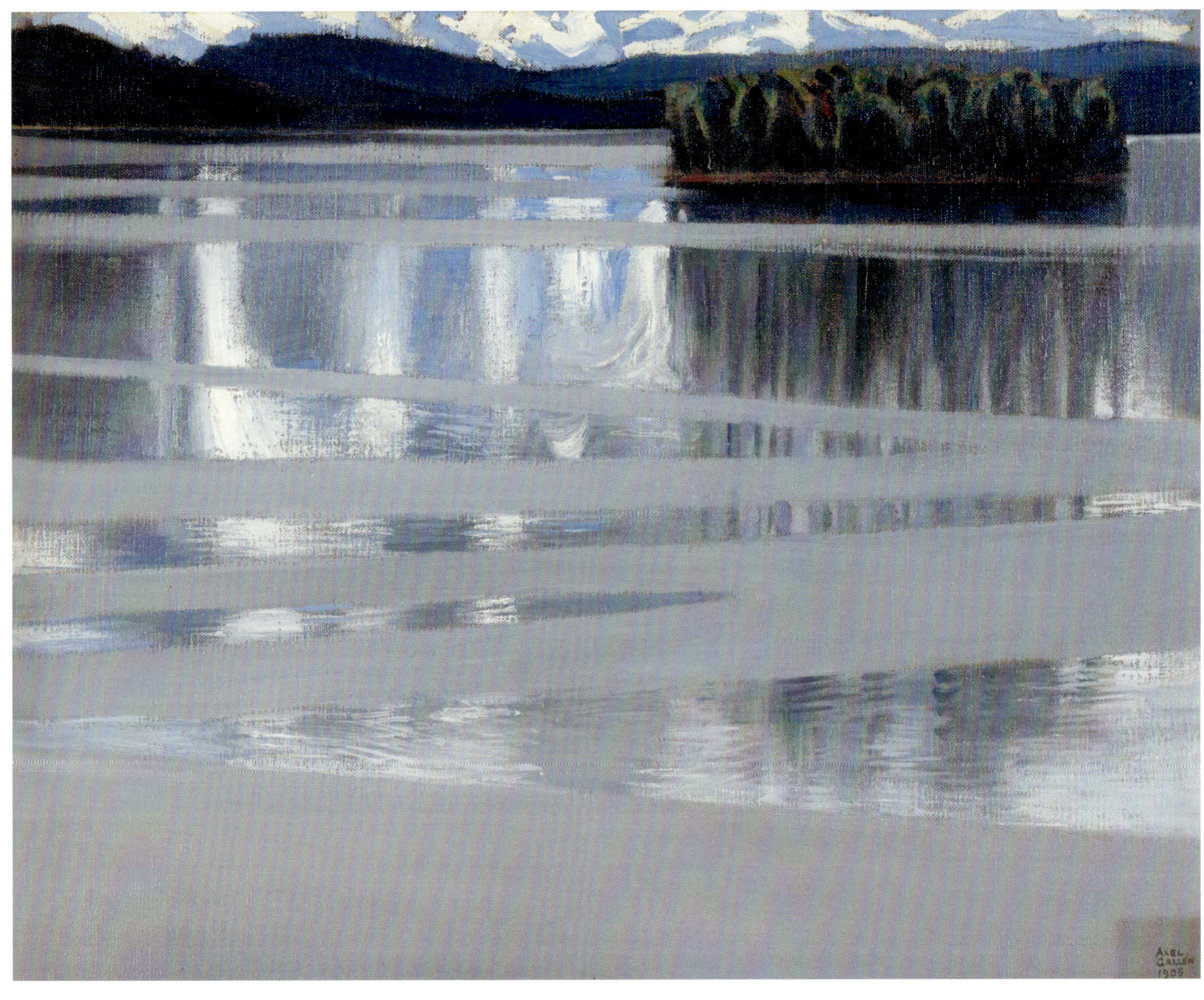

Cat. 7

Akseli Gallen-Kallela
Lake Keitele, 1905

Oil on canvas, 53 × 66 cm
The National Gallery, London (NG6574)

Exhibited in Helsinki as early as 1905, the year of its completion, this version of the Lake Keitele landscapes is likely to be the first of the four versions to have been put on public display.[1] In fact, it might have been with this intention in mind that Gallen-Kallela adjusted the composition, creating a more naturalistic appearance: it is suffused with light, reverting to the atmosphere observed in the portrait of Mary of 1904 (cat. 4). The abstract, monochrome block in the lower part of the two other versions of the painting (cats 5 and 6) has given way to a liquid, realistically depicted foreground of quivering wavelets. Thus modified, the landscape looked less harshly modern and disconcerting, and the work was no less attractive.[2] However, the daring network of steel-grey bands criss-crossing the surface of the lake still imposes its presence. Dominating each of the four Lake Keitele versions, these patterns are caused by winds combined with currents below the water. Close to nature and eminently sensitive to the effect of weather fluctuations on the landscape, Gallen-Kallela examines these with particular accuracy. Yet he provided his own interpretation of this meteorological curiosity, giving us clues for its correct understanding: these are the traces of Väinämöinen's boat, the old, wise bard and central character of the *Kalevala*, who has just rowed past, leaving a silvery wake; these 'silvery stripes at the surface of the serene water are the wavelets announcing the passions to come', Gallen-Kallela wrote.[3] It may also have evoked the trips on the lake he would often take in his rowing boat (replaced that summer by his first motor boat, *Jolanda*, on which he made painting trips)[4], just like the great *Kalevala* hero, a parallel and possible identification Gallen-Kallela would no doubt have relished. In 1904–5, the *Kalevala* legends on which he had constructed his reputation, and to which he owed his growing fame (the first monograph devoted to the artist was written in 1904), were still haunting him; he was in the process of working on more paintings – and illustrations – completing his *Kalevala* cycle as the Lake Keitele landscapes were under way. Of all his compositions based on the great Finnish epic, this is undoubtedly the most allusive and abbreviated.

1 The Finnish Art Society spring exhibition at the Ateneum, Helsinki, 10 May 1905.
2 It appears the painting soon, probably barely a few weeks after its completion, entered the collection of the news agency founder Woldemar Westzynthius (1858–1905) who died on 30 March of that year. The 1905 spring exhibition at the Ateneum, Helsinki, included paintings from the recently deceased Westzynthius.
3 Strasbourg 1999, p. 156.
4 Simonaho 2012, pp. 56–69.

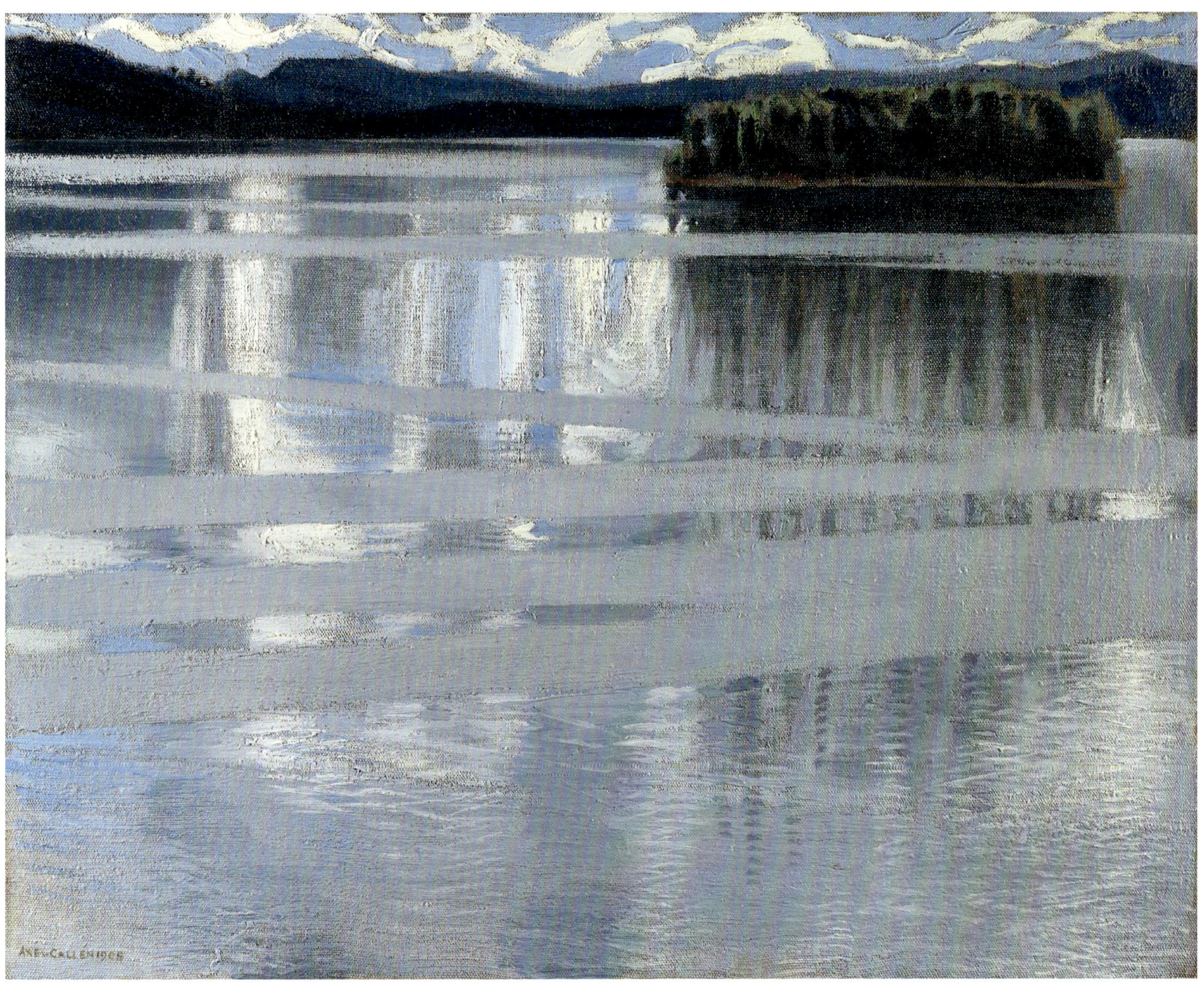

Cat. 8

Akseli Gallen-Kallela
Lake Keitele, 1906

Oil on canvas, 59 × 74 cm
Private collection

Thought to be the fourth and last version of the Lake Keitele land-scape paintings, this work incorporates the alterations implemented by the artist in the picture now in the National Gallery, London (cat. 7). It is also the largest. Its foreground shows the waters of the lake being quietly ruffled by the wind, described by subtly entwined brushstrokes, conjuring up the soft music of lapping wavelets. The painting looks to be dated 1906, the late winter months of which Gallen-Kallela spent in Suolahti, taking part in lynx hunts, a stay that may have rekindled memories of his time spent at nearby Konginkangas two years earlier.[1] This canvas may have been executed for purely commercial reasons.[2] The maintenance of the Kalela studio house consumed much of the family's funds, and although he was by then a successful artist, Gallen-Kallela's works were still often produced as the result of financial necessity: for example, in 1906 he accepted commissions for advertising posters.[3] In the past year, Finland's political situation had become tenser than ever; the artist's signature to the lower left of the painting is an indication of his unfaltering determination to support the nation-alist cause. While a native Swedish speaker, Gallen-Kallela made a point of speaking Finnish, sometimes artificially so; we are told that his Finnish sounded quaint and outdated. Likewise, motivated by an exacerbated awareness of his Finnishness, he soon preferred using the Finnish form of his name to sign his works: Gallen-Kallela as opposed to the Swedish-sounding Axel Gallén, the name by which he had been known until then. 'Gallen-Kallela' had a strong Finnish consonance and it also harked back to the use by Renais-sance artists of the name of the place from which they originated: Axel Gallén's ancestors came from Kallela in western Finland. The artist's self-fashioned name, and signature, signalled his commit-ment to the fight towards Finnish independence and his ideological support of the cause.

1 A manuscript note by the artist dated 29 November 1907 (at the Gallen-Kallela Museum) reveals Gallen-Kallela committed to paint a version of Lake Keitele 'during the year 1908'. Experts at the Gallen-Kallela Museum have wondered whether this might be the painting in question, despite the date reading '1906'.
2 It entered the collection of the powerful Swedish-Russian Nobel family, wealthy industrialists, related to Alfred Nobel, who founded the Nobel prize.
3 Helsinki 1996, p. 23.

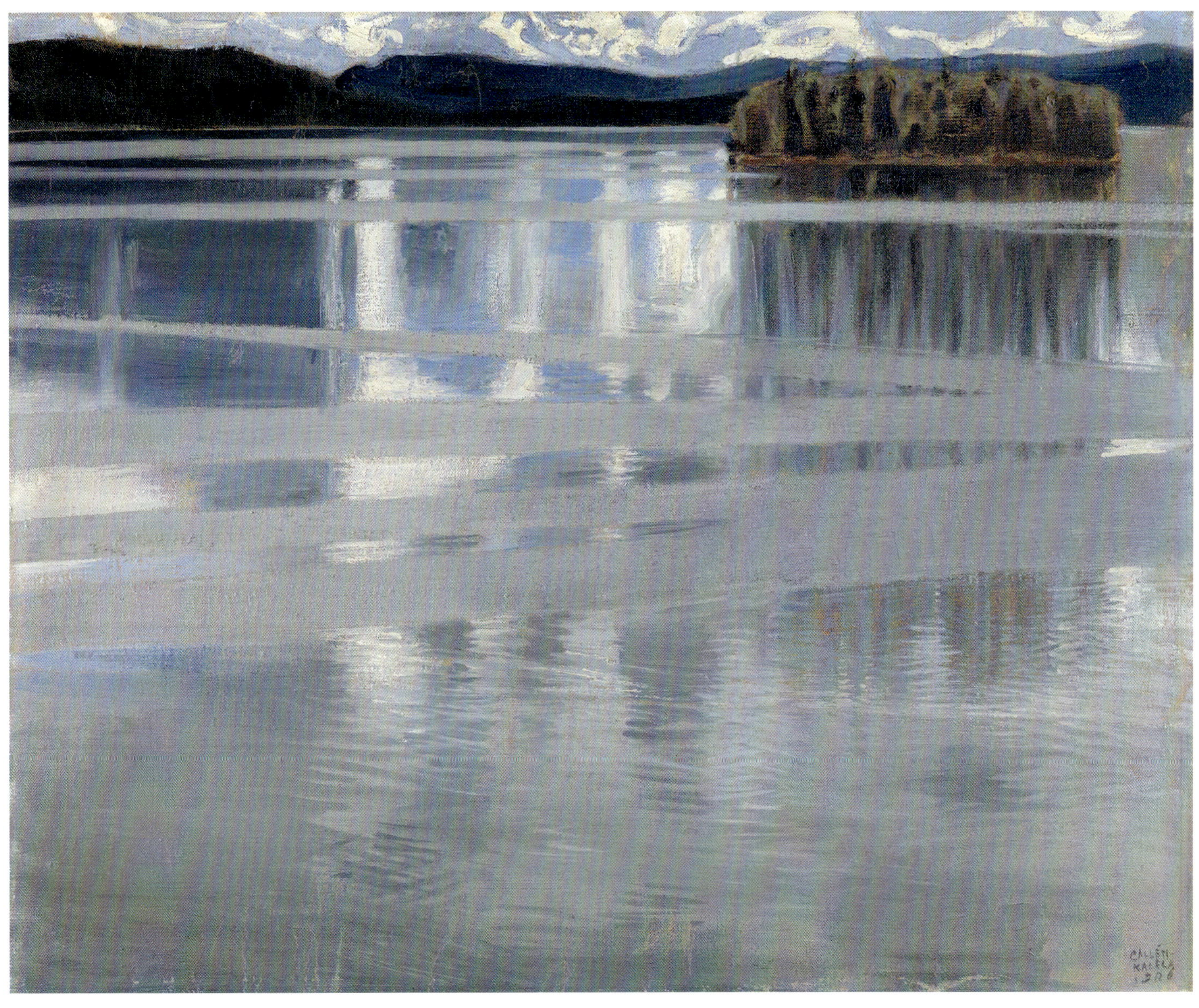

Cat. 9

Akseli Gallen-Kallela
Clouds, 1904

Oil on canvas, 64 × 64 cm
Didrichsen Art Museum, Helsinki

Another view of Lake Keitele is here offered for our contemplation. We are invited to explore it from a different, slightly higher point of view: from an elevated spot that, as a result, lowers the landscape's horizon line, positioned dramatically high in the four Lake Keitele compositions. The square canvas is divided horizontally into two almost equal areas of sky and water, separated by the green line of the island and distant shore. Seascape and cloudscape are granted equal importance, offset by the elegant asymmetry of the island's dark green mass to the right of the picture, and the spectacular 'cloud towers' (a title by which the painting is sometimes known) reflected on the surface of the water. The weeks spent at Lintula Villa in the summer of 1904 coincided with a phase of creative insecurity. They followed Gallen-Kallela's 'great fresco period',[1] which started in 1899 with his murals for the Paris World Fair's Finnish Pavilion, and finished in the summer of 1903 with the completion of the Jusélius mausoleum frescoes, which absorbed most of his time and energy for several years. The Paris frescoes had been demolished with the pavilion, a temporary structure; the Jusélius decorations had started to deteriorate barely a year after their completion due to the moisture in the mausoleum's walls; and illness had affected Gallen-Kallela while travelling abroad: all elements that prompted a time of doubt and depression. The idyllic surroundings of Lake Keitele helped the artist recover his creative energy. His desire to renew himself is manifest here, in this inventive composition executed with aplomb, using a heavily loaded brush. Monumental clouds are scudding in the sky, forming a spectacular canopy of summer cumuli, contrasting with the limpid, crystalline surface of the lake below.

1 Martin and Sivén 1985, p. 70.

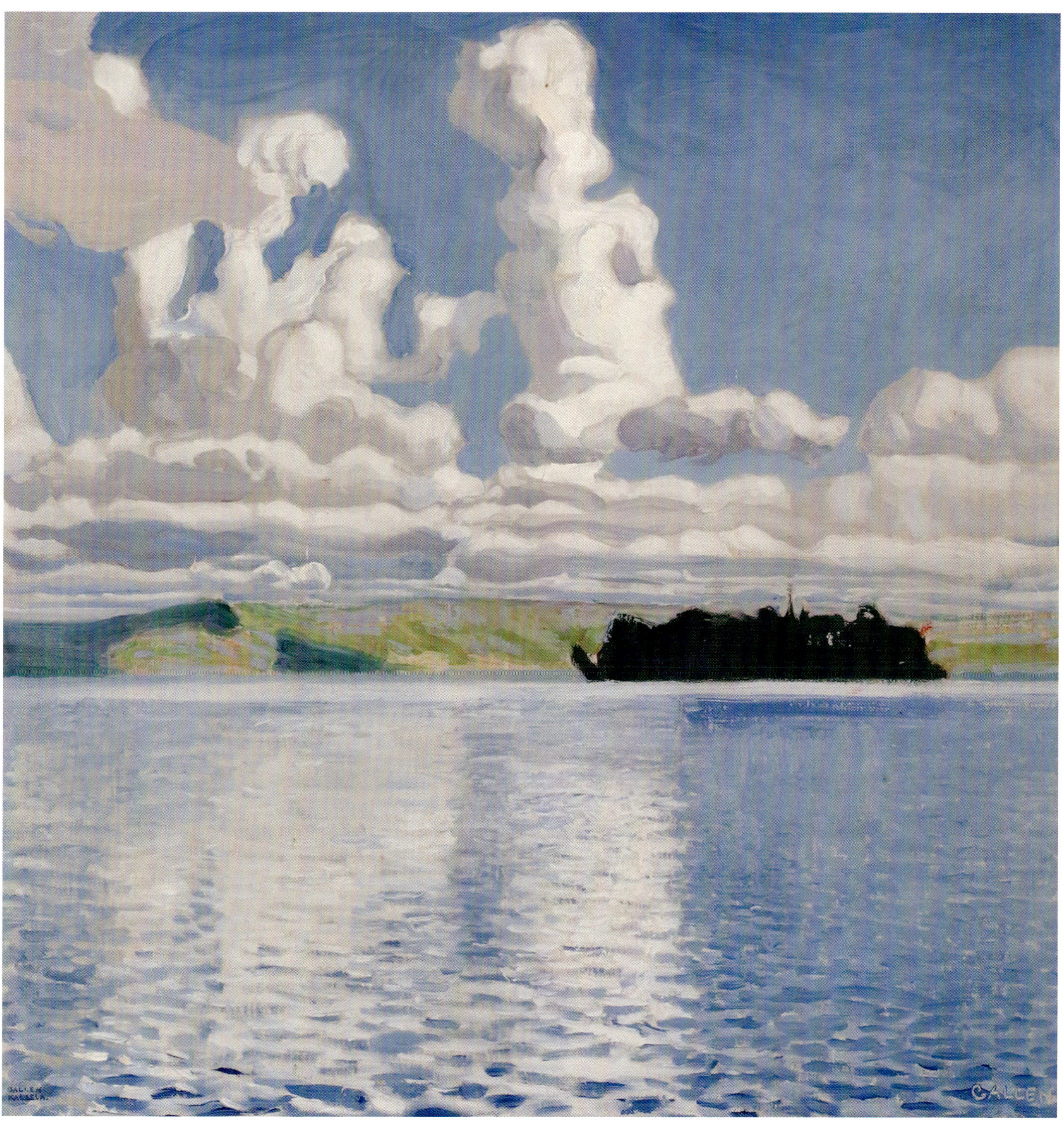

GALLÉN-KALLELA.
GALLÉN

Cat. 10

Akseli Gallen-Kallela
Clouds above a Lake, 1904–6

Oil on canvas, 52 × 55 cm
Gallen-Kallela Museum, Espoo, Finland

In this sublime landscape, Gallen-Kallela pursues further the compositional formula tested in his *Clouds* (cat. 9); the horizon line is in the middle of the canvas here, creating a mirror effect in which the sky and lake oppose each other in an electrifying tension. The wooded island is now in the centre, punctuating the image and providing a firm anchoring point. From the painting emanates a baroque energy and elemental, almost cosmic, grandeur, as well as a sense of intense agitation and turbulence: as though a peaceful, sunny afternoon was about to be disrupted. The balletic frieze of clouds is turning into a gaping, mysterious and possibly sinister hole, with the threat of a storm looming in the distance. Gallen-Kallela may have intended the painting as a metaphor for the country's climate of political unrest, as its simmering desire for freedom from Russia, for autonomy and power was intensifying. Heavy clouds, broken branches, burnt forests and smothering piles of snow start to dominate in Gallen-Kallela's paintings of this period, following the political troubles:[1] the murder of the Russian Governor General in 1904 and the 1905 General Strike. The country was suffocating under Russian oppression; in this context, *Clouds above a Lake* can also be read as a beacon, a glimmer of hope in Finland's struggle for independence, anticipating imminent and economic freedom from Russia.

1 Helsinki 1996, pp. 270–1, 274.

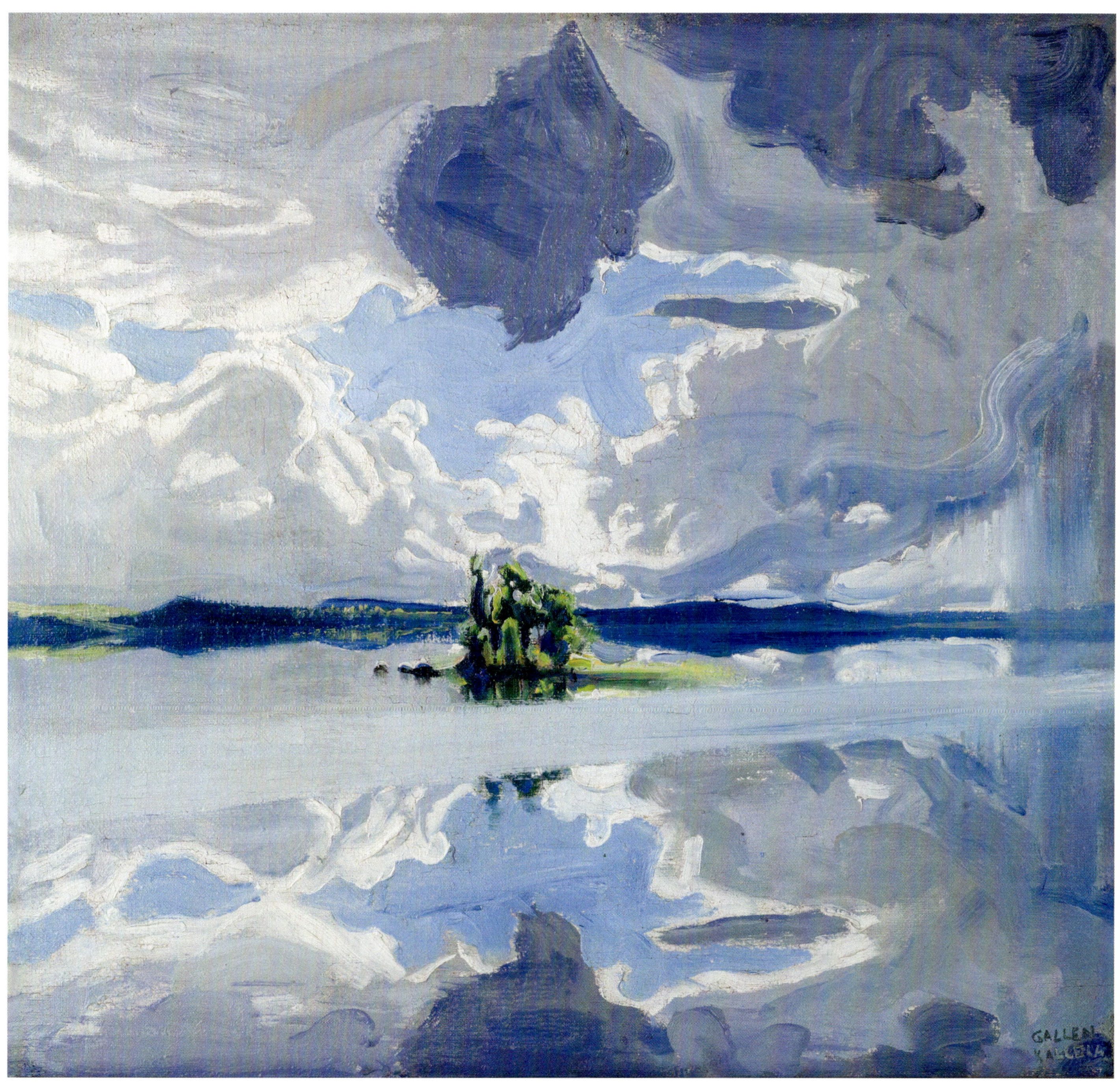

Cat. 11

Akseli Gallen-Kallela
Väinämöinen with Maidens, 1905

Oil on canvas, 44 × 64 cm
Private collection Grankulla, Finland

Gallen-Kallela had a lifelong interest in the *Kalevala*, from which he started to seek inspiration in the 1880s. Following a trip to rural Karelia in 1890, where the poems originated and were still being sung, *Kalevala* subjects dominated the works he produced over the next 10 years. Before long he was recognised as the principal illustrator of these ancient legends of Finland. By translating them into visual form, he created a distinctive imagery, presenting the nature and folk life of Finland from a long-gone mythical age in a powerful epic style. Founded on ethnographic references, Gallen-Kallela's 'heroic' *Kalevala* paintings show a solid, simplified and stylised grandeur in perfect accord with the spirit of the Finnish runes. By the mid-1900s he was still tackling ambitious canvases based on the *Kalevala* legends, notably the *Departure of Väinämöinen* on which he had been working for a decade. This painting was conceived initially as a triptych, but was eventually condensed into a single canvas featuring the final adventures of the mighty Väinämöinen.[1] The *Kalevala*'s central figure, the 'combined Mercury and Orpheus of the Finns, inventor of fire, boat and lyre, guardian of all the arts', Väinämöinen captivated Gallen-Kallela with his exploits.[2] *Väinämöinen with Maidens*, a preliminary thought for a composition of which several versions exist, shows the old bard leaving in 'a boatload full of maidens':[3] a more literal, less allusive transcription of the rune. The lake is the location for the last episode of this river journey; the dark, pointed trees of its island, so crucial to the *Lake Keitele* composition, are just visible, their reflection interrupted by the luminous streak delineated by the wake of Väinämöinen's vessel. His copper boat, dramatically cropped, glows with warm hues, prolonging the rapidly brushed silvery criss-cross. The white summer light falls on the girls' torsos, illuminating their golden locks and diaphanous skin. Sitting at the prow, chin in hand, Väinämöinen looks pensively at the naked maidens. Gallen-Kallela described him as a 'powerful yet sad figure represent[ing] the eternally burning, clarified and high passion of life. The innocent lack of self-awareness of the young girls represents the throbbing power of spring'.[4] The mood is melancholic and lyrical as the hero is shown meditating on the girls' youth, and on his journey, maybe as an echo to Gallen-Kallela's own desire to sail 'away to loftier regions, to the land beneath the heavens'.[5]

1 Strasbourg 1999, p. 170 (cat. 61); Groningen 2006, pp. 148–9.
2 Karkama, 2008, p. 125.
3 Ilvas 1996, p. 156 (letter referring to a study for the 1909 *Väinämöinen's Journey*).
4 Gallen-Kallela, in Espoo 2011, p. 37.
5 *Kalevala*, Rune 50.

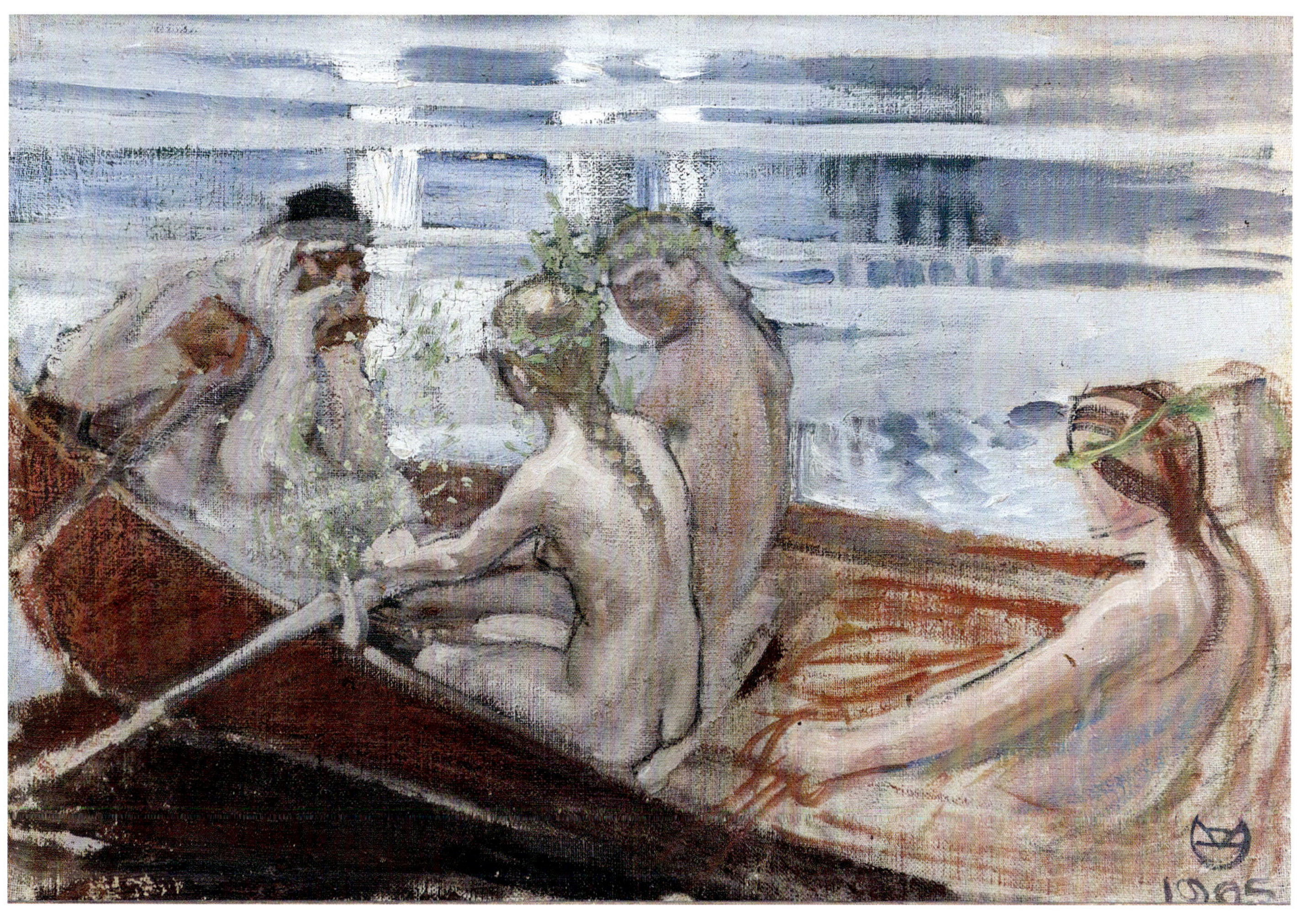

Akseli Gallen-Kallela
Oceanides, 1909

Oil on canvas, 53.5 × 73 cm
Finnish National Gallery, Ateneum Art Museum,
Helsinki, Finland, Wäinö Walli Collection

In the early part of 1909 Gallen-Kallela was living in Paris, working fervently on a number of canvases destined for the city's Salon d'Automne: 'Instead of sinking into ordinary solitude, in a sterile examination of conscience', he wrote, 'my inner self has opened like a flower and immediately expressed itself in forms and colours – especially colours, as the result of which I painted without ceasing'.[1] This burst of creativity resulted in *Oceanides*, another *Kalevala* fantasy, for which this painting is a study. In bright sunshine, the sea gives birth to the maidens; their joyous dance imposes its dynamic, primal strength, causing the water to ripple. Graphic shapes are delineated on the water's iridescent surface, as if the rhythmical zigzags observed in the Lake Keitele landscapes were disintegrating around the maidens' bodies. Gallen-Kallela defined his faceless Oceanides by their flamboyant colours: 'five naked girls eagerly swimming in an inland lake, with golden sand on the bottom and the blow glimmer of the sky on the surface, totally yellow and blue – nothing else'.[2] Intense and ecstatic, the work signals a new use of colour in his oeuvre, as his palette lightens and brightens. Although vehemently critical of the latest developments of modern art, Gallen-Kallela kept a close eye on other artists' formal experiments and on the major changes underway, which he witnessed at first hand while in Paris.[3] At this time, he had become a member of Die Brücke, although his artistic affinities with the German avant-garde group would prove weaker than anticipated. At the 1905 Salon d'Automne, the Fauves had caused a stir and Paul Cézanne's posthumous retrospective in 1907, which included his large *Bathers*, had been a watershed. Exuding vitality, Gallen-Kallela's *Oceanides* and his other outdoor compositions painted in 1909 have been described as 'Gallénian Fauvism',[4] but may rather be linked to different, more classically subdued currents in contemporary French painting, such as the decorative works of Maurice Denis, who was well represented at the 1909 Salon d'Automne. A few months later Gallen-Kallela was to embark on a trip with his family on a steam ship from Marseille to East Africa. *Oceanides* also announces the colourism of his African period, and the new mode of expression he was to develop there.

1　Letter to Johannes Öhquist, 2 April 1909, in Paris 1998, p. 38.
2　Letter to Johannes Öhquist, autumn 1909, in Espoo 2011, p. 111.
3　He criticised Matisse's paintings, but remained preoccupied with him, enquiring in letters about him and wondering what he was painting (to Johannes Öhquist, 25 October 1910, from Africa; the Gallen-Kallela Museum Archives, Espoo).
4　Olli Valkonen, in Espoo 2011, p. 110.

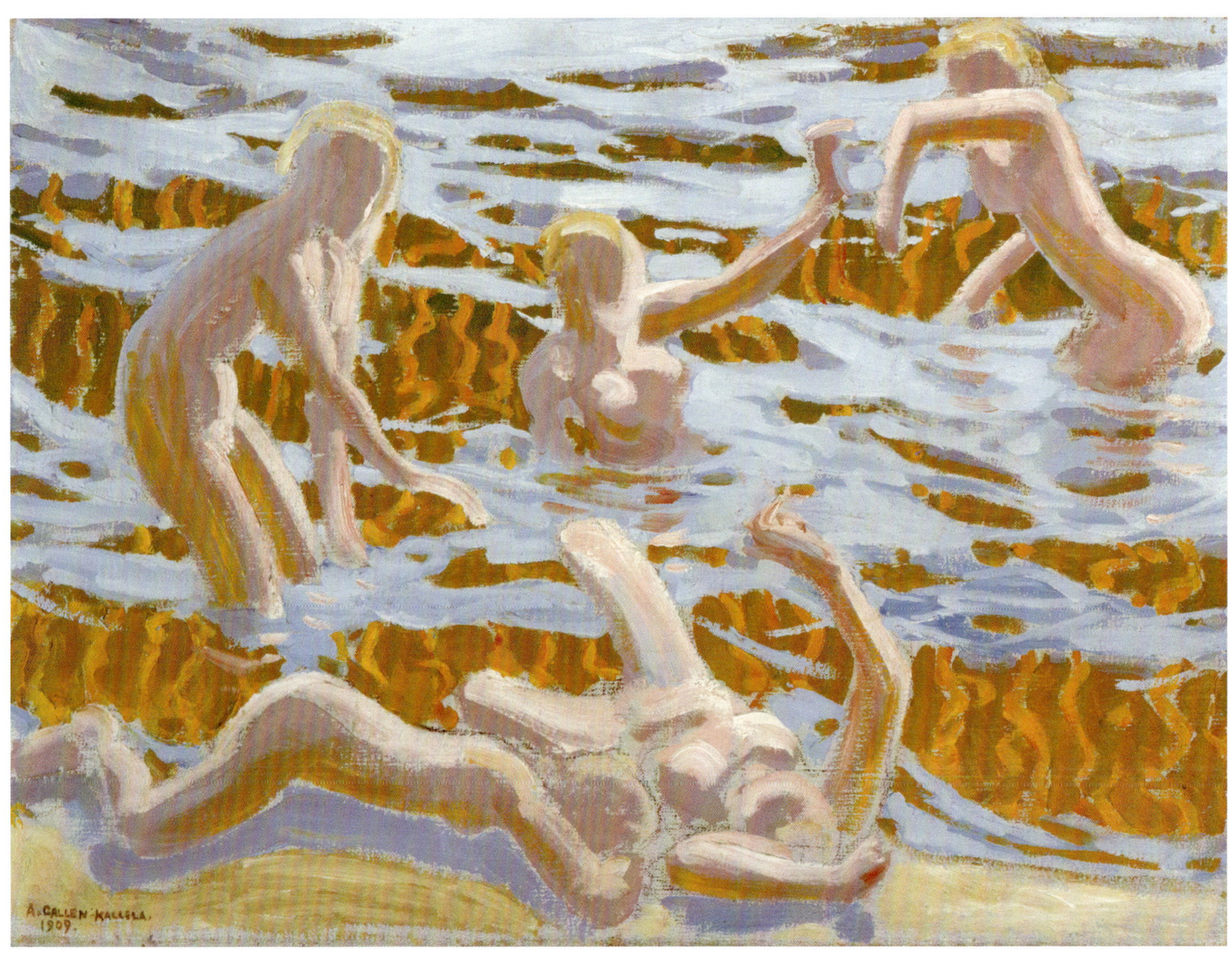

Cat. 13

Akseli Gallen-Kallela
Lakeside Landscape, 1915

Pastel, 97 × 100 cm
Private collection

By 1915, Gallen-Kallela's reputation was at its highest; his work had just been exhibited at the Venice Biennale and was being shown in America for the first time.[1] Back home, he had embarked on a new project: the construction of Tarvaspää, his 'studio-castle' outside of Helsinki, designed and built like a medieval fortress, where the family settled in 1913. In 1915, after celebrations in honour of his fiftieth birthday, they decided to leave the area, where Russian soldiers were intensifying their presence at this time of political unrest; the family moved back to Ruovesi. The location of Kalela (the studio he kept running alongside Tarvaspää), and the scenic views of Lake Ruovesi it offered, no doubt brought reminiscences of his many lakeside paintings of a decade earlier (fig. 22). There, he painted more such views of dramatic landscapes with striking effects of light at sunset.[2] Amid the political turmoil, these pictures were likely to have acquired new connotations, as images symbolising Finnish national self-consciousness; the artist remained strongly attached to his country, aesthetically and emotionally. This is also where he probably executed this pastel, newly discovered and undoubtedly linked to his Lake Keitele compositions. Gallen-Kallela had worked in pastel in the late 1880s, in portraits and landscapes – some of them studies, some of them equally large and highly accomplished – not least a lakeshore scene of peasants embarking on a boat;[3] his mastery of the medium was evident. In *Lakeside Landscape*, with hatched streaks and swirling strokes, and a restricted palette of bluish tints, the artist achieves spectacular chromatic effects in the glistening water and incandescent sky. He repeats the Lake Keitele motif, rather than records the observed scenery at Ruovesi, allowing it to expand on a larger and squarer format, as if seen from a wider angle. A diffuse, evanescent mist surrounds the landscape, evoking an enigmatic world of memories, a mysterious serenity. The dreamlike ambience links it back to Symbolism and the visionary landscapes of the celebrated French pastellist Lucien Lévy-Dhurmer (1865–1953), Gallen-Kallela's contemporary. Here, the image has retained its astonishing impact; its colours glow and the whole surface shimmers, enhanced by the medium's powdery quality. As he wrote, 'The older I get, the more strongly I yearn – for what? I will tell you: [...] for light so powerful that the sun blackens, and for colours that sparkle and explode'.[4]

1 *Panama-Pacific International Exhibition*, San Francisco, California, 1915.
2 *Sunset over Lake Ruovesi*, 1915–16, Sotheby's London, 20 November 2012, no. 29; *Spring Ice as seen from the Roof of Kalela*, 1916, in Groningen 2006, p. 129.
3 *Midsummer's Eve*, 1889, pastel, 102.2 × 56 cm, Ateneum, in Helsinki 1996, p. 167.
4 Martin and Sivén 1985, p. 201.

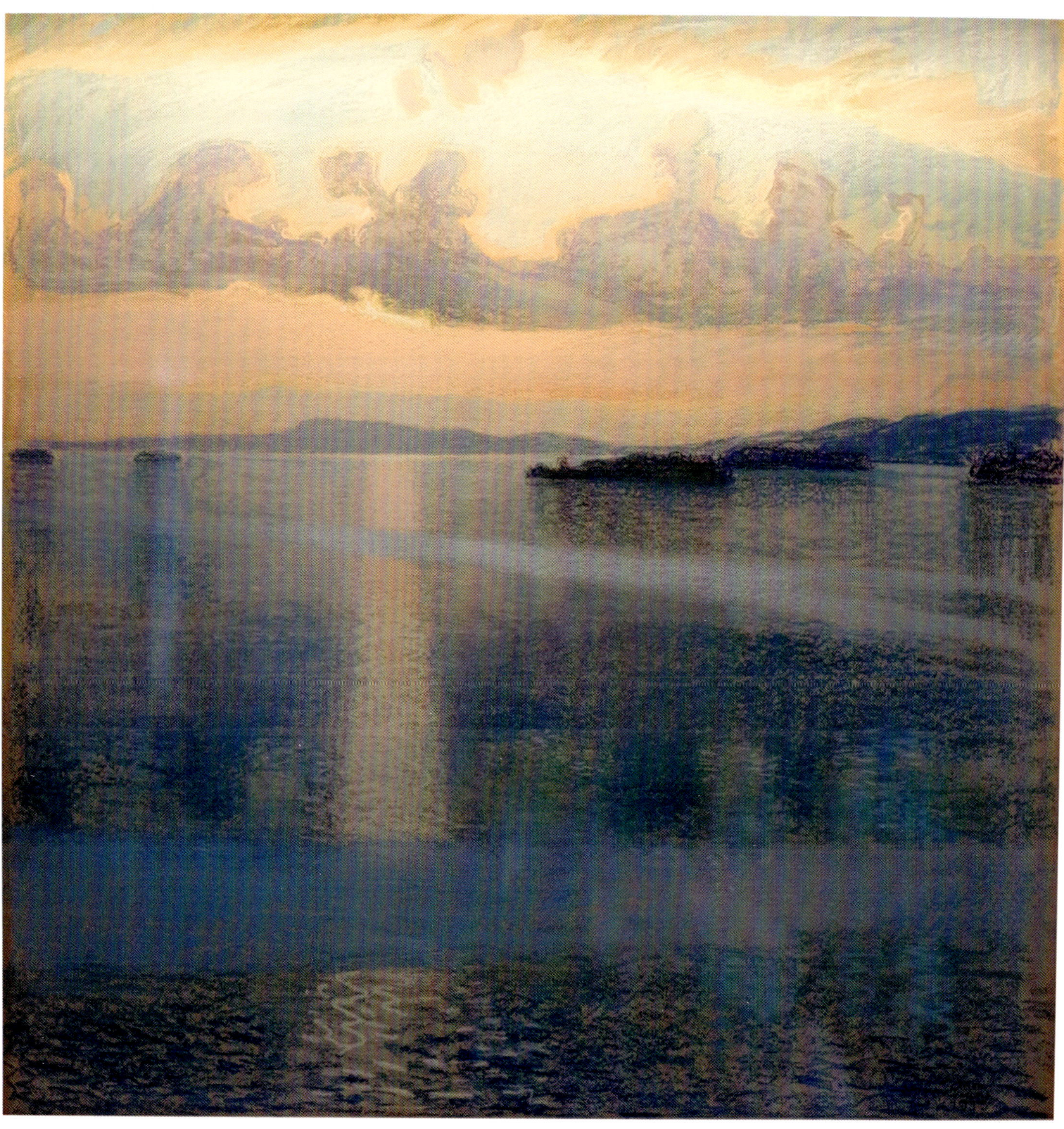

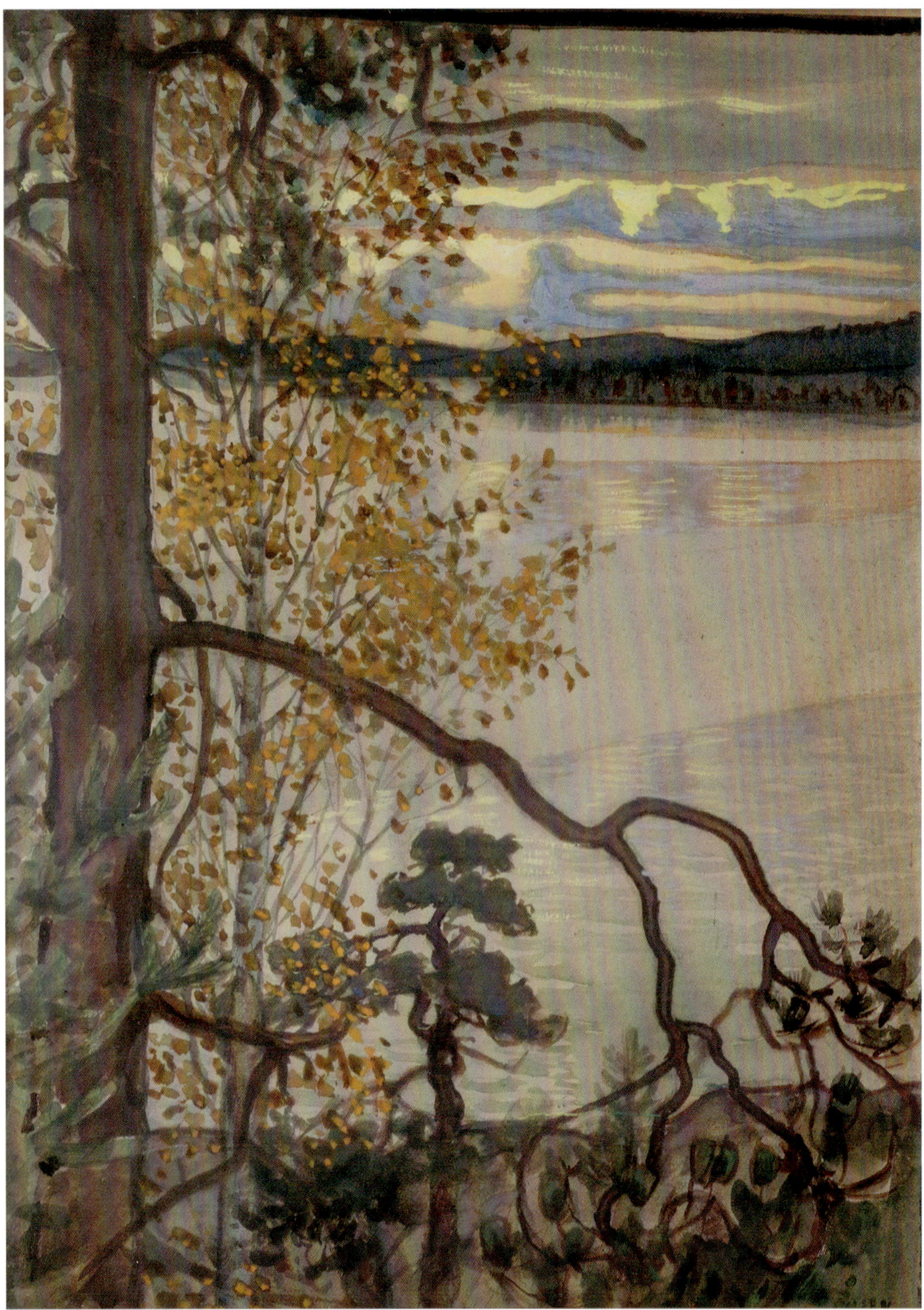

Fig. 22   **Akseli Gallen-Kallela**, *View from Ruovesi*, 1898
Watercolour on paper, 34 × 25 cm
Collection Sigurd Frosterus/Amos Anderson Art
Museum, Helsinki

Notes

1 Groningen 2006; Paris 2012; Paris 2015.
2 Groningen 2006, p. 33.
3 At the Académie Julian, Gallen-Kallela studied in William-Adolphe Bouguereau's and Tony Robert-Fleury's studios.
4 Helsinki 1996, p. 108.
5 Okkonen 1948, p. 21.
6 Ilvas 1996, p. 142.
7 Gallen-Kallela, to his mother, 22 December 2003: 'Je pars en janvier via Stockholm, Copenhague et Berlin, Vienne, puis Munich et Paris où j'ai l'intention de passer l'hiver en m'exerçant à peindre d'après un modèle vivant; je pense tout recommencer, comme un écolier' [I leave in January via Stockholm, Copenhagen and Berlin, Vienna, then Munich and Paris where I intend to spend the winter by practising painting from a life model; I intend to start everything over like a school child], quoted in Paris 1998, p. 37.
8 To Fru Thyra Neovius, Paris, 21 June 1888. Ilvas 1996, p. 105.
9 1886 (Gallen-Kallela's first trip to central Finland), Helsinki 1996, p. 36, footnote 28.
10 To Edvard Neovius, 2 August 1890. Ilvas 1996, p. 112.
11 To Fru Thyra Neovius, Ekola farm, Keuru (central Finland), 1 February 1887. Ilvas 1996, p. 104.
12 The painting was exhibited at the Galerie Durand-Ruel, Paris, in 1887.
13 *Kalevala*, Rune 50. First English translation by John Martin Crawford, 1888.
14 Jansson 2008, p. 157.
15 Quotation from Gallen-Kallela's sketchbook for 1899. Groningen 2006, p. 45. Also Coleman 2014, p. 12, footnote 23.
16 To Edvard Neovius, Visuvesi, 27 August 1891. Ilvas 1996, p. 144.
17 Juhana G. Linsén, Chairman of the Finnish Literature Society, quoted in Wilson 1976. Also Coleman 2014, p. 12, footnote 20.
18 Ilvas 1996, p. 98.
19 Martin and Sivén 1985, p. 10; Groningen 2006, p. 2; Paris 2012, pp. 22–4.
20 Strasbourg 1999, p. 40.
21 Brooklyn 1982, p. 14. 'Developments in Scandinavian painting from 1880 to 1910 do not conform to the sequence of stylistic progress we know so well from the often-described evolution of French Impressionism and Post-Impressionism.' Also Coleman 2014, p. 13, footnote 50.
22 At Salon Ugo Barroccio, Berlin, from 3 March 1895.
23 Hagelstam 1904.
24 His large landscape, *Frühjahr*, [Spring] (1900), was acquired by the Moderne Galerie, Vienna (now Belvedere) in 1901.
25 Coleman 2014, p. 7, footnote 51.
26 Olli Valkonen spoke of 'Gallenian Fauvism'. Espoo 2011, p. 110.
27 To Pekka Halonen, 3 March 1909. Ilvas 1996, pp. 154–5.
28 Paris 2012, p. 24, footnote 11.
29 Gallen-Kallela's Journal, 1893, in Coleman 2014, p. 8, footnote 62 (translation).

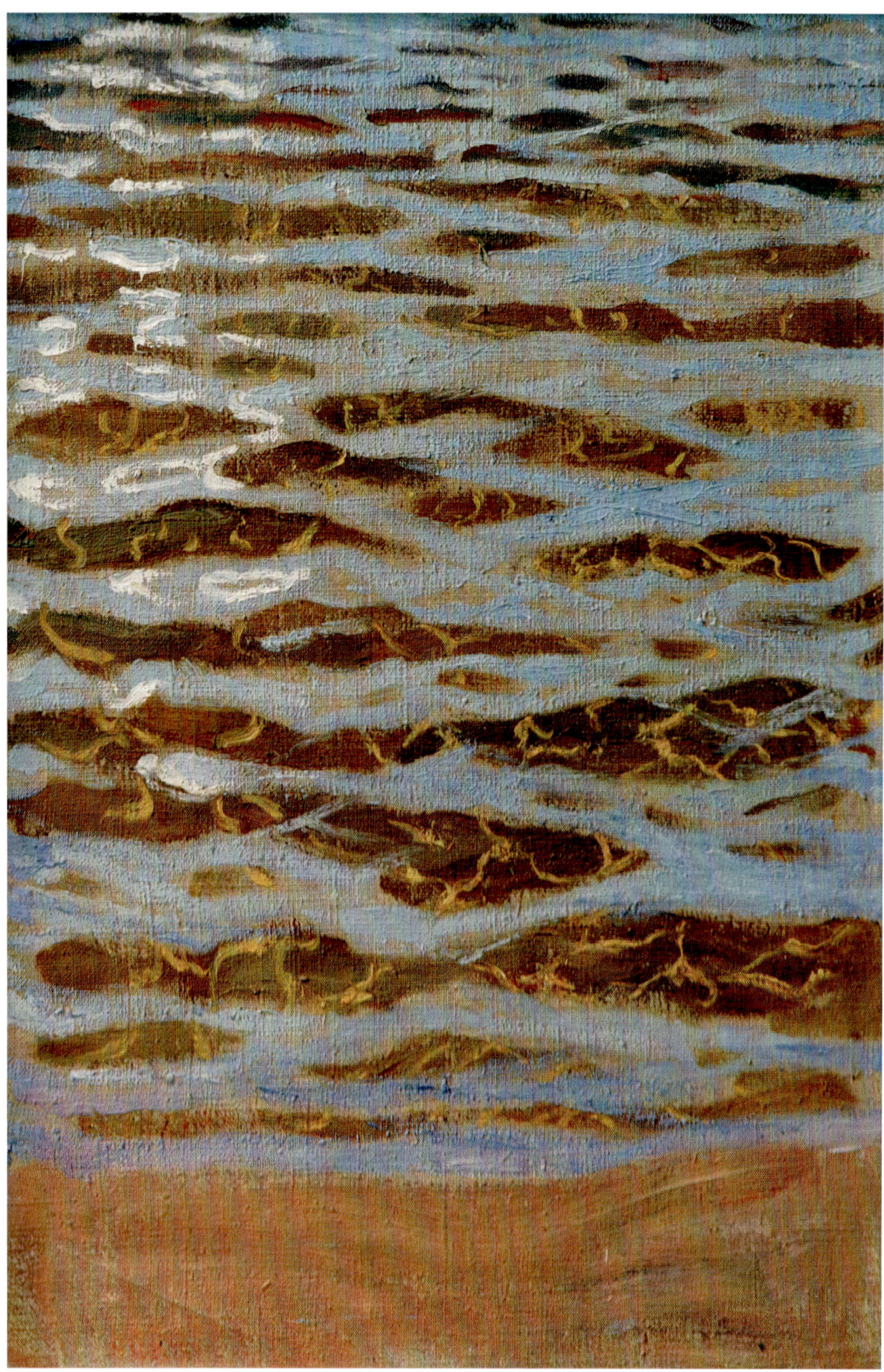

Fig. 23   **Akseli Gallen-Kallela**, *Waves*, 1893
Oil on canvas, 62 × 42 cm
Private collection

Bibliography

Amsterdam 2012
Rodolphe Rapetti, *Dreams of Nature: Symbolism from
Van Gogh to Kandinsky*, exh. cat., Amsterdam, Van Gogh
Museum and Mercatorfonds 2012

Brooklyn 1982
Kirk Varnedoe, *Northern Light*, exh. cat., New York City,
Brooklyn Museum 1982

Coleman 2014
William L. Coleman, 'Sibelius, Gallen-Kallela, and the
Symposium: Painting Music in Fin-de-Siècle Finland',
Nineteenth-Century Art Worldwide, vol. 13, issue 2,
Autumn 2014

Copenhagen 2006
Torsten Gunnarsson, *A Mirror of Nature: Nordic Landscape
Painting 1840–1910*, exh. cat., Copenhagen, Statens Museum
for Kunst 2006

Espoo 2011
Tuija Wahlroos (ed.), *Fill your Soul! Paths of Research into the
Art of Akseli Gallen-Kallela*, exh. cat., translated by Jüri
Kokkonen and Valerie Vainonen, Espoo, Gallen-Kallela
Museum 2011

Gallen-Kallela 1955
Akseli Gallen-Kallela, *Kallela-kirja*, Helsinki, Werner
Söderström Osakeyhtiö 1955

Gallen-Kallela-Sirén 2005
Janne Gallen-Kallela-Sirén, 'The "Sacred Spring" of National
Art: Axel Gallén and the Image of Finland', *Belvedere:
Zeitschrift für bilden de Kunst*, vol. 1, 2005

Groningen 2006
David Jackson (ed.), *Akseli Gallen-Kallela: The Spirit of
Finland*, exh. cat., Groningen, Groninger Museum & NAI
Publishers 2006

Groningen 2012
David Jackson (ed.), *Nordic Art – The Modern Breakthrough*,
exh. cat., Groningen, Groninger Museum & Hirmer Verlag
2012

Hagelstam 1904
Wenzel Hagelstam, *Axel Gallén: En studie*, Stockholm 1904

Helsinki 1996
Ilvas Juha (ed.), *Akseli Gallen-Kallela: Ateneum*, exh. cat.,
Helsinki, Finnish National Gallery Ateneum 1996

Helsinki 2001
Timo Huusko, *Surface and Depth: Early Modernism in
Finland 1890–1920*, exh. cat., Helsinki, Finnish National
Gallery Ateneum 2001

Helsinki 2004
Leena Ahtola-Moorhouse (ed.), *Albert Edelfelt 1854–1905:
Jubilee Book*, exh. cat., Helsinki, Finnish National Gallery
Ateneum 2004

Helsinki 2014
Tuija Wahlroos (ed.), *Akseli Gallen-Kallela & Berlin.
Die Historischen Schichten der Gemälde*, exh. cat., Helsinki,
Gallen-Kallela Museum 2014

Ilvas 1996
Juha Ilvas, *Sanan ja tunteen voimalla: Akseli Gallen-Kallela
kirjeita/A Self-Portrait in Words: The Letters of Akseli
Gallen-Kallela*, Helsinki, Finnish National Gallery 1996

Jansson 2008
Mats Jansson, Janna Kantola, Jakob Lothe and H. K.
Riikonen (eds), *Comparative Approaches to Nordic and
European Modernisms*, Palmenia, Helsinki University Press
2008

Karkama 2008
Pertti Karkama, 'Kalevala ja kansallisuusaate', *Kalevalan
kulttuurihistoria*, SKS [Finnish Literature Society] 2008

Martin and Sivén 1985
Timo Martin and Douglas Sivén, *Akseli Gallen-Kallela,
National Artist of Finland*, Helsinki, Watti-Kustannus Oy 1985

Okkonen 1946
Onni Okkonen, *Finnish Art*, Helsinki, Werner Söderström
Osakeyhtiö 1946

Okkonen 1947
Onni Okkonen (ed.), *Gallen-Kallela Piirustuksia/Teckningar/
Drawings*, Helsinki, Werner Söderström Osakeyhtiö 1947

Okkonen 1948
Onni Okkonen, *Akseli Gallen-Kallelan Taidetta*, Helsinki,
Werner Söderström Osakeyhtiö 1948

Paris 1998
Suzanne Pagé (ed.), *Lumière du monde, lumière du ciel*,
exh. cat., Paris, Musée d'art moderne de la Ville de Paris
1998

Paris 2012
Fabienne Chevallier, Janne Gallen-Kallela-Sirén, Laura
Gutman-Hanhivaara, Magdalena M. Moeller and Philippe
Thiébaut, *Akseli Gallen-Kallela. Une passion finlandaise*,
exh. cat., Paris, Musée d'Orsay 2012

Paris 2015
Suzanne Pagé (ed.), *Keys to a Passion*, exh. cat., Paris,
Fondation Louis Vuitton, Yale University Press 2015

Pettersson 2016
Susanna Pettersson (ed.), *Stories of Finnish Art*, Helsinki,
Finnish National Gallery Ateneum & Hatje Cantz 2016

Raivio 2005
Kaari Raivio, *Akseli Amerikassa: Akseli ja Mary
Gallen-Kallelan kirjeen vaihtoa vuosilta 1915–1931*,
Helsinki, Werner Söderström Osakeyhtiö 2005

Simonaho 2012
Helena Simonaho, 'Gallen-Kallela ja Konginkangas',
Kongintaival, *Konginkangas*, Konginkankaan kotiseutukerho
ja Kömin Kilta ry, 2012

Strasbourg 1999
Rita Ojanperä (ed.), *L'Horizon inconnu: L'art en Finlande
1870–1920*, exh. cat., Strasbourg, Musées de Strasbourg,
Galerie de l'Ancienne Douane & Ateneum 1999

Strengell 1906
Gustaf Strengell, *Finska mästare: Edelfelt, Järnefelt, Gallén.
En gruppbild*, Helsinki, Helios 1906

Vienna 2005
Stefan Koja (ed.), *Nordic Dawn. Modernism's Awakening
in Finland 1890–1920*, exh. cat., Vienna, Österreichische
Galerie Belvedere 2005

Wilson 1976
W. A. Wilson, *Folklore and Nationalism in Modern Finland*,
Bloomington, Indiana University Press 1976

List of Lenders

Espoo, Finland
Gallen-Kallela Museum: cats 2, 10

Helsinki, Finland
Didrichsen Art Museum: cat. 9
Finnish National Gallery, Ateneum Art Museum: cats 1, 3, 12

Lahti, Finland
Lahti Art Museum/Viipuri Foundation: cat. 6

Private collections
We would like to thank the private collectors who wish to
remain anonymous: cats 4, 5, 8, 11, 13

Photographic credits

BASEL
Kunstmuseum Basel © akg-images/De Agostini Picture Lib.: fig. 11.

BUDAPEST
Szépművészeti Múzeum, Budapest © Szépművészeti Múzeum, Budapest/Scala, Florence, photo Jozsa Denes: fig. 18.

ESPOO
Gallen-Kallela Museum © Gallen-Kallela Museum: fig. 4; © Gallen-Kallela Museum/photo Hannu Aaltonen: cat. 2; © Gallen-Kallela Museum/photo Katja Hagelstam: cat. 5; © Gallen-Kallela Museum/photo Jukka Paavola: cat. 10; figs 2, 8, 17; © Gallen-Kallela Museum/photo Petri Summanen: fig. 12; © Gallen-Kallela Museum/photo Tuukka Uusitalo: cat. 4.

HELSINKI
Amos Anderson Art Museum Amos Anderson Art Museum/photo Stella Ojala: fig. 22.
Didrichsen Art Museum © Didrichsen Art Museum, Helsinki: cat. 9.
Finnish National Gallery, Ateneum Art Museum © akg-images/De Agostini Picture Lib./A. Dagli Orti: fig. 21
Finnish National Gallery © akg-images: figs 5; © Photo: Finnish National Gallery/Kirsi Halkola: cat. 3; © Photo: Finnish National Gallery/Janne Mäkinen: cat. 12; © Photo: Finnish National Gallery/Pirje Mykkänen: cat. 1; © Finnish National Gallery/Ateneum Art Museum, Helsinki/Bridgeman Images: figs 15, 19.
Mannerheim Museum © Mannerheim Museum, Helsinki/photo Matias Uusikylä: fig. 21.

LAHTI
Lahti Art Museum/Viipuri Foundation © Archive of the Lahti City Museum/photo Tiina Rekola: cat. 6.

LONDON
© Tate, London: fig. 14.
© The National Gallery, London: cat. 7.
© Victoria and Albert Museum, London: fig. 20.

PARIS
Musée d'Orsay, Paris © RMN-Grand Palais (musée d'Orsay)/Hervé Lewandowski: fig. 13.

PRIVATE COLLECTIONS
© akg-images: figs 1, 3, 6, 10, 23.
© photo courtesy Bukowskis, Helsinki: fig. 7.
© Photo courtesy of the owners: frontispiece, cats 8, 11, 13; fig. 9.
© Photo Fanny Haga: cat. 11.

TURKU
Turku Art Museum © akg-images: fig. 16.

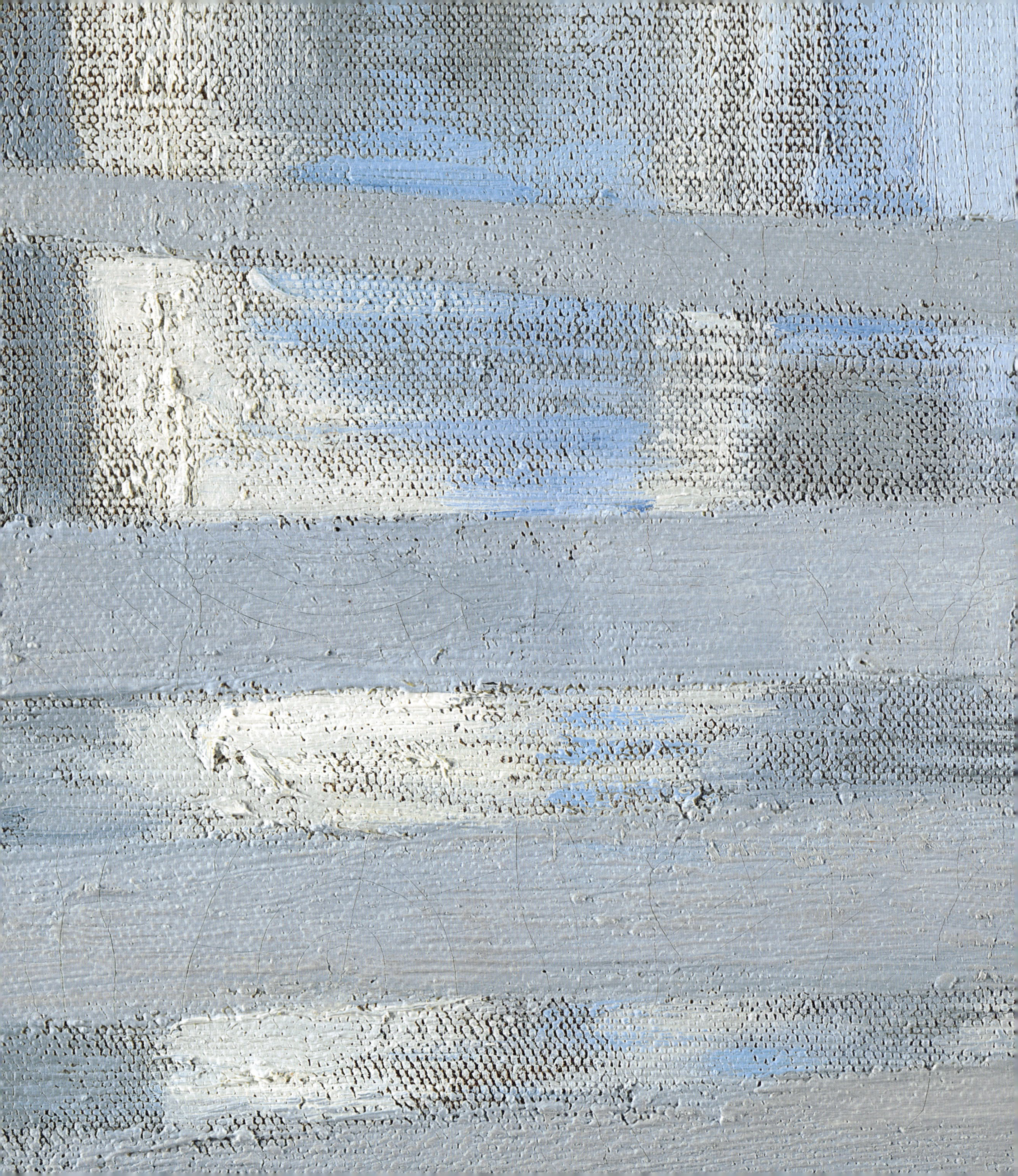